Praise for The

"An insightful, enjoyable book that offers the kind of instant payback that's critical to anyone working in a fast-growing, entrepreneurial business. It challenged me to look closely at myself, how I operate and how that plays out with others. In doing so, I discovered that – despite my best intentions – sometimes my attempts to help others aren't actually that helpful. This deepened my understanding of my relationship with my boss and ways to further improve it. It also enabled me to adapt my approach to leading others."
Michael Borthwick, Group Financial Controller at Claranet

"An incredibly useful and accessible book that has transformed my thinking and approach to both managing upwards and leading my team. As a leader, it's crystal clear to me that the relationships I have with my team are critical to the success of the work we do together. The ten 'lessons' described in this book offer us a way of examining and discussing those relationships to set us all up for success. It's a book I know I'll read and refer to more than once and the author makes that easy: there's a lot to reflect on and the way *The Boss Factor* is written is like having him in the room with you."
Simon Haskey, Consulting Practice Lead at Dell EMC

"Richard Boston has nailed it. If only I'd known this earlier in my career, I'd have saved myself a lot of grief, done a much better job, and had a happier boss! With so many books for leaders and so few for those they lead, this will be invaluable for anyone in their first or second job, as well as for those in middle management looking to enhance their relationships upwards."
Peter Young, Director and executive coach at Bladon Leadership

"Insightful, practical, enjoyable and accessible. There are a lot of books out there, many of them hard to finish. This one hooks you in with a combination of stories, facts, ideas, theory and challenging exercises that encourage the reader to pause and reflect on what the content really means for them. As much as you'll want to read on, it's well worth investing some time in that reflection: you'll remember more, you'll apply more, and you'll find the various questions and exercises trigger powerful conversations with your boss and any people you lead."

Rebecca Stevens, whose previous roles include heading up leadership, talent and organisational development at Kimberly-Clark, Deloitte and BP

"A really important book on a really important topic. Every one of us has a boss: even as a CEO I had people who could call me up in the middle of the night and make demands of me. The great leaders are the ones who've lived up to Richard Boston's ten lessons when working with the people above them – whether they've done so by accident or by design. This book will save you the pain of learning the hard way. It'll help you craft your own, informed recipe for success. And it's a really easy read: I like it so much I've already read it twice and will no doubt come back for more."

Tony Cooper, retired Partner at Deloitte, entrepreneur and ex-CEO of Merryck & Co

"I had a great time reading this book. When I first read it, I was a few months into a new in role in a complex, pressured environment and it took some of that pressure off. It's an interesting and enjoyable read, rich with new ideas and material, and was directly relevant to conversations and challenges I was having at the time. Not only that, it challenged my assumptions about what it means to lead and be led. It helped me see patterns I'd built up over the years. It encouraged me to be honest with myself and it got me thinking differently about myself, my boss, team and peers; about the relationships between us; and about the world in which we operate."

Catherine Poyner, Head of Transformation in central government

"A refreshing book that takes a new perspective on the relationship between leaders and the people they lead. I really loved the practical tools and exercises, which made this book a directly relevant, interactive and memorable experience where so many are a passive stroll through theories that are all too easily forgotten. This book actually made me think far beyond just reading it. It made me do something. It made it stick."

Geoff Morey, Learning and Organisational Development Consultant at Macmillan Cancer Support

"An inspirational and highly enjoyable read... especially given the current situation in my career, having just moved into a new role, in a new team, with a new manager, in a new company. I have always been intrigued by the fact that, across a range of jobs, I have sometimes struggled with my bosses while at other times things went really, really smoothly. This book offered some powerful insights into why that is and encouraged me to reflect on what I bring to those relationships. I am sure many, many other people will enjoy it as much as I did!"
Vicky Monsieurs, HRD Manager, Center Parcs Belgium-Netherlands-Germany

"I took a lot of value from this book both as a leader and as a follower of leaders. It also felt realistic, showing that Richard Boston understands that it's not possible to be perfect in either role at all times. It has helped me become a better boss for the people I lead and has inspired me to change the way we work as a team. Like most leaders, I cannot be successful without the people I lead. This book has helped me begin to create an environment that's intentionally designed to enable a team to excel in their roles, get the best from me and allow room for growth. I'd recommend it to other leaders, either as a book to give to your people, as a reference point for one-to-ones and team meetings, or as a blueprint to use behind the scenes."
Mark Griffiths, Director of Account Relationship Management at WorkForce Software

"A very useful, highly educational book that distils a huge amount of knowledge and a multitude of methodologies into a format that is very easy to digest and apply. Each chapter stands alone and provides its own concise guidance. However, the greatest value is in the whole: this is a book that challenges stereotypes, looking at leadership from the other side of what is after all a two-way relationship. By understanding and applying the book's 10 lessons we enhance our understanding of both sides of that relationship, which can only enhance our ability to lead."
Seb Henkes, founder of Sabio, a multi-award-winning tech company listed as one of the UK's best places to work

"A concise, eminently readable book that offers an interesting counterpoint to the mass of books written on leadership. It made me challenge myself – especially on

the topic of courage in the relationship with one's boss. As a 'middle manager' I've found it helpful to combine this new book with insights from the author's previous book, *ARC Leadership*, to ensure a 360° approach to my workplace relationships. Highly recommended."
Matt Champkin, Recruitment Manager at Blick Rothenberg

● ● ●

Praise for Richard's previous book, ARC Leadership

"This book has had a real impact on me... Business schools in particular would do well to pay attention... given what's gone on in corporations, they need to take greater responsibility for producing future leaders who aren't simply able to profitably grow a business, but are – to their core – Authentic, Responsible and Courageous."
Karen Lombardo, recently retired Worldwide Head of Human Resources at Gucci Group

"A rigorous, intelligent book that challenges us to make a fundamental shift, to make ourselves better – both as leaders and as people."
Adam Burns, Editor, MeetTheBoss TV

"Positive, hopeful, intelligent, friendly, shrewd, eye-opening, evidence-based and incredibly generous. It challenges and supports us like a great coach or trainer would do... part character review, part campaign for personal overhaul."
Phil Hayes, Chairman, Management Futures

● ● ●

THE BOSS FACTOR

RICHARD BOSTON

Cover design: Objective Ingenuity
Production: Alison Rayner

Published by LeaderSpace
Harwood House, 43 Harwood Road, London SW6 4QP
All enquiries to: publications@leaderspace.com

First published 2018

ISBN: 978-0-9929445-3-7 (Paperback)
ISBN: 978-0-9929445-5-1 (eBook-ePub)
ISBN: 978-0-9929445-4-4 (eBook-Kindle)

For Evie

Contents

•●•

What role are the processes and structures around you playing in enhancing or limiting your capacity to deliver?

What contribution will you need to make to building the capacity of others?

How your commitment will have a tangible impact on your performance

What is it, exactly, that you should be committing to?

Who else's commitment is critical to your success?

How to manage your own commitment and that of your boss and key stakeholders

How courage is key to delivering on each of the lessons in this book

What do we mean by 'courage' in the workplace?

What happens when courage and commitment collide?

How to boost your courage – both temporarily and for the longer term

Why you and your boss will thrive by promoting these lessons in others

What are you and your boss role-modelling for others?

How can you create a culture that recognises and rewards the habits and mind-sets at the heart of this book?

How to select, enable and encourage people who create genuine, mutual value in their relationship with their boss

BRINGING IT ALL TOGETHER

What we've covered

What you've learned

What you're doing differently

Where to from here?

THREE MONTHS ON

What's happened since you last picked up the book?

What successes have you had?

Where have you stalled or relapsed?

How might you have used this book differently if, when you started, you knew the things you know now?

• ● •

APPENDICES

This book in a nutshell

●◉●

- Why read this book?

- Why these 10 lessons?

- How best to approach them

- How it all hangs together

THIS IS A BOOK ABOUT YOU and the person or people who lead you, whether you call them your boss, your manager, your director, the CEO, the permanent secretary, the non-execs, your senior stakeholder(s), sir, madam, your highness or something else.

It's not a leadership book, although it'll help make you a better leader – whether you're an experienced leader, a newcomer or aspiring to a leadership role. It's designed to help you thrive. For you that might mean earning more money, progressing faster up the career ladder, breaking through a plateau or out of a rut, improving a bad or less-than-optimal relationship with your current boss, becoming their most trusted second-in-command, or simply doing ever-more interesting work and having a great deal more fun. The single most important 'factor' that you can influence that'll determine whether your boss helps or hinders your attempts to thrive? The relationship between you and them.

> "None among us is always a leader and never a follower"
>
> Barbara Kellerman[1]

This isn't about thriving at your boss's expense, though. This isn't a collection of tips or tricks that'll enable you to manipulate your boss into doing whatever you want. The intention here is to develop a genuine, mature and mutually beneficial relationship based on trust, healthy challenge and clear, aligned objectives.

This is a book that'll give you a fresh and practical perspective on your relationship with one of the most important people in your life right now. It'll challenge you to re-evaluate your own expectations and assumptions with regard to that relationship, and to take responsibility for your role in making that relationship a success. It'll offer you insights into your boss's ways of thinking and working, and how those complement and clash with your own. It'll help you choose the right leader for you, and ensure you and your boss (or bosses) are clear on what each of you expects from the other. It'll help you broaden your remit, develop your skills and make sure you've the resources and processes in place to deliver on what's expected of you. If you use this book as it's intended, you'll find it gives you a greater sense of purpose, satisfaction and contribution. Depending on what you're doing already, the actions you take out of it could enhance the respect and/or admiration you get from others. You'll also be putting in place a way of working that contributes positively to your mental health[2].

It's also a book that will put the onus on you to be proactive, self-aware and increasingly intelligent when it comes to understanding the people who lead you. Make no mistake, this is not a book about sitting back, passively, and waiting to be led. It's about taking responsibility for the single most important 'boss factor' you can influence.

All but the most dysfunctional bosses will appreciate you living up to the ten 'lessons'* in this book. For starters, you'll be helping free them from the temptation to micro-manage you, enabling them to find better ways to add value to the organisation. As organisations face conditions and environments that are increasingly 'VUCA' (volatile, uncertain, complex and ambiguous), we are increasingly required to distribute power, decision-making and information processing across teams and organisations,

---

* I use the term 'lesson' because these are lessons I've learned and am keen to share

rather than concentrating them in the hands of a few. Your boss is only going to be able to do that if they have high-quality people supporting them who can take a greater share of their responsibilities.

If you're also a leader in your own right, the ten lessons in this book will also provoke you to think differently about the conditions you create for the people you lead. One reader restructured his team and its workflow, reallocating roles and responsibilities, changing the nature of his one-to-ones with them and revising the interview questions he used to recruit new team members. Others have questioned how well they're role-modelling healthy, mature ways of working with their seniors, and whether they're expecting the people they lead to treat them better than they're treating their own bosses.

We'll get to those ten lessons shortly. First, it's important to put those lessons in context. So I'll tell you about the business school professor whose (frankly irritating) exhortation prompted me to write this book. I'll then touch briefly on the ways this crucial 'boss' relationship varies across the changing world of work.

The business school prof who started it all

A few years ago, I was a faculty member sitting in a lecture theatre at a prestigious business school helping run an international leadership programme for fifty participants. Beneath us, addressing three semicircles of participants, was one of the school's distinguished professors. He was – and still is – a man I both like and respect, who's highly intelligent and oozes gravitas, but he made a throw-away comment that really made me angry. Not just irritated, but angry enough to write this book.

"This is a leadership programme," he said. "If you want the followership programme, it's next door."

It wasn't, of course. There was no followership programme on offer at that business school, nor any other business school as far as I knew. Why would there be? Why would *anyone* sign up for a course that would teach them how to *follow* others?

There's a three-pronged paradox here, though. Firstly, leaders are utterly reliant on the people they lead. Leaving aside the fact that they can't really call themselves leaders if no one's following, if the people they lead don't deliver, the leader can't deliver. So, arguably, good followership is at least as critical to a leader's, team's and organisation's performance as good leadership.

Secondly, it's practically career suicide to refer to oneself as 'a great follower'. Until I wrote this book, no client I'd ever known or heard of had ever requested a followership development programme. This suggests we have a massive lack of respect for people who make an art of having exceptional relationships with their bosses, but at the same time we are utterly reliant on virtually everyone being good at it. In spite of those high expectations, and because of that lack of respect for this other side of leadership, organisations offer very little support, guidance or training in how to operate on that other side. Even in the military, often credited with developing both sides of the leadership relationship, there's recognition that 'followership development' needs more attention[3]. So it's no surprise that the hundreds of leaders, managers and executives I've worked with are so often seeking help with their upwards relationships.

Virtually all of us have a boss

The third prong of the paradox is this: virtually every leader is also led by someone else. If we respect one side of the leadership relationship more than the other, does this mean we respect and value those people more when they're facing down the hierarchy than when they're facing up it? Surely we shouldn't, should we? Certainly, the direction they're facing will often affect their behaviour, but surely we (and they) should value their ability to do a good job of facing up the hierarchy, too?

One of the first people to read this book was a CEO. On reading it, he realised that his behaviour was changing when he went into meetings with his chairman because he'd "changed hats". When we discussed the book he said "It reminded me of the need to be aware of that subtle change and bring my leadership behaviours into that upwards relationship. If I don't, then I'm being less effective in my role as a leader of the organisation *and* when I'm effectively being 'led' by the non-execs."

Not all CEOs and their staff recognise that the chairman or chairwoman is in many ways the CEO's boss.

What if I have more than one boss, a rapid succession of bosses, or I'm not even sure who my boss is?

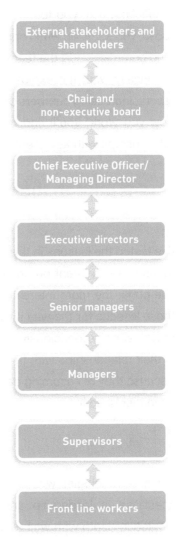

In traditional, relatively stable hierarchies resembling the example on the right, bosses are easy to spot. If you work in a matrixed organisation, with two or more 'bosses', the lessons in this book will apply to all of those relationships. If you work in teams that form and disband fairly quickly (e.g. on a succession of short projects), then I'd argue that these lessons are even more important to you: with a greater sense of urgency and less time to get to know your boss, you'll want to apply the lessons quickly to maximise your chances of a successful outcome in the work you're doing together.

We're also seeing a shift towards Agile teams and 'holacracy', where people have multiple roles that are defined around work streams rather than individuals, and where teams evolve frequently to keep up with changing demands. Many of these teams are self-organised and authority is distributed in a less traditional way. They're characterised as 'flat', devoid of hierarchy. However, it's human nature that there's almost always a boss or two – emergent, unofficial leaders to whom the rest of the team defer. So, if you're in that kind of environment, it could be an unofficial 'boss' you focus on when reading this book. Alternatively, the 'boss' you focus on when applying these lessons could be the stakeholder who commissioned the team to do the work in the first place.

Finally, with the explosion of the 'gig' economy and crowdsourced labour, increasing numbers of people are operating as freelancers. If that's how you work, you'll find many of these lessons apply equally well to relationships with key clients.

Where in the hierarchy do I need to be to get maximum value from this book?

I've tested the lessons in this book at all levels and done my best to avoid focusing the content on one particular slice of the hierarchy. The higher I've gone, the more interested people have been on the implications of those lessons for the way they lead. In some cases, that's been because they're already consciously or unconsciously applying some of the lessons in their relationships with their own bosses. In other cases, I suspect it's because they're assuming development is for other people, and that they no longer need it.

Where do these ten lessons come from?

I'm a psychologist whose training began in 1990. Since I chose to specialise in leadership and team performance, back in 2000, I've worked in depth with well over a thousand leaders at all levels in diverse organisations on six continents and across the private, public and not-for-profit sectors. I've worked less closely, less extensively, with a couple of thousand more, right down the hierarchy to the front line – observing how they operate, assessing their performance and contributing to their development. So this book blends psychological research and theory from the realms of leadership, team dynamics and followership* with the lessons I've learned helping clients with challenges they've had with their bosses, their colleagues and the people they lead. Naturally, I've also been influenced by my own experiences of leading and being led.

As the first few lessons took shape, I realised they were new expressions of principles I'd been developing in my work on leadership and team performance. At the core of that work lie Three Core Disciplines that sum up the things leaders, teams and organisations need to *do* in order to be sustainably successful:

- Establish a clear Direction – drawing on their own aspirations and the needs and expectations of those around them

- Secure Commitment to that direction – both internally and from the individual's, team's or organisation's key stakeholders

- Build sufficient Capacity to deliver on that direction – again, both internally and externally.

---

* Where I'm drawing on the work of others or particular pieces of research, I'll provide the relevant references – and sometimes further explanation – at the back of the book. Previous readers have preferred that to me naming all of my sources as I go, which they said breaks the flow of the text. I'm keen to give credit where credit is due, though. So I've also named my biggest influences in the Acknowledgements at the end of the book.

These Three Core Disciplines apply to any endeavour, whether we're working as individuals, teams or organisations. Not only that, but if individuals, teams, their leaders and their organisations – those three central triangles – aren't aligned then neither they nor the system around them will be functioning as well as they could be.

Delivering on those Three Core Disciplines isn't easy, though. We live in complex times and each of us is fairly complex in our own right. Conflicts and competition between our own habits, needs, beliefs, expectations and assumptions* and those of others make it hard to Establish a Direction that pleases everyone, to Secure their Commitment to it, and to ensure we have sufficient Capacity to deliver on everyone's expectations.

To channel this complexity in a way that enables rather than inhibits our ability to deliver on the Three Core Disciplines, my book *ARC Leadership*[4] argues that most of us need to be increasingly Authentic, Responsible and Courageous (the three ARC Qualities for which the book is named).

When we're Authentic, Responsible and Courageous we understand, take responsibility for, and challenge our own existing mind-sets. We take responsibility for ensuring all stakeholders' needs are met, not just our own, which shapes a more comprehensive and sustainable Direction, while at the same time securing more people's genuine Commitment to it. We're prepared to be bolder when choosing that direction, stretching ourselves and others, and we hold each

---

* For simplicity, I'll typically group beliefs, expectations and assumptions under the term 'mind-sets'.

other to account for our individual and collective roles in fulfilling it. We authentically assess our current capacity to achieve that vision, then take courageous responsibility for filling any gaps and unlearning any habits that risk constraining that capacity and reducing our chances of success.

It's this framework, combining the ARC Qualities with The Three Core Disciplines, that underpins these ten lessons. The intention throughout is to help you create the conditions in your relationship with your boss that enable you to be Authentic, Responsible and Courageous with them, with yourself and in the rest of your work and relationships. That way, together, you'll deliver on the Three Core Disciplines.

The ten lessons

Lesson 1 helps you establish your own authentic direction, informing Lesson 2 where you'll be assessing the alignment between your boss's chosen direction and your own, as well as their potential to secure and maintain your commitment, build your capacity and enable you to be authentic, responsible and courageous.

Lessons 3 and 4 explore your needs and mind-sets, how those might align and clash with your boss's, and the impact that's having on both of you.

Lesson 5 offers you a framework for agreeing a clear direction and degrees of autonomy when taking on work from your boss. Lesson 6 encourages you to reassess and redefine your responsibilities, helping you step up without over-reaching or undermining your relationships with key stakeholders.

Lessons 7 and 8 explore your role in continually building capacity and ensuring that you, your boss and your shared stakeholders stay sufficiently committed to deliver optimal outcomes.

Lesson 9 focuses on the need for courage and the tensions that can arise between being courageous and being committed.

Lesson 10 challenges you to help others deliver on the previous nine lessons, to create a culture around and beneath you in which everyone takes due responsibility for healthy, successful relationships with the people who lead them.

Which lessons tackle *habits*? All of them. You'll be invited throughout to challenge your existing habits in search of more effective ones.

Why do none of these lessons tell you to "get great results"? Because:

- It's too obvious and if you need a book to tell you to get results you're probably not my target audience

- Your results are an *outcome* and this is a book about the *inputs* that will achieve that outcome and others

- If you're more focused on your own individual results than on the ten lessons in this book, you'll be less of an asset than people who are.

How well do these lessons transfer across cultures?

Different cultures hold different norms when it comes to the relationship between a leader and the people they lead. Russia is generally far more hierarchical, for instance, than the USA, which makes it harder to bring the challenge that's required to help Russian bosses avoid falling foul of group-think. This also means, arguably, that Russians are more courageous than Americans when they bring that upwards challenge. People from Britain and Australia are on average far more individualistic and less focused on collective success than the average Brazilian or Chinese person[5], which makes it harder for British and Australian workers to demonstrate collective responsibility and to buy into the concept of making their boss successful, unless it's clearly and tangibly in their own best interests.

In spite of these differences and the local nuances they bring, the Three Core Disciplines still apply, as do those three enabling or inhibiting forces (habits, needs and mind-sets) and the three ARC Qualities.

How to use this book

Cover-to-cover or back and forth?

Some people like to read books from cover to cover; others dip in and out. So, while there's a logic to the order in which I've placed the ten lessons, this book is also designed for people moving back and forth, following their interests and targeting the lessons that feel most useful at the time. I've done my best to make each lesson stand alone, although the whole is definitely greater than the sum of its parts.

Reading as a leader in your own right

If you're a leader in your own right, it'll be hard for you not to consider how each lesson might apply in your relationships with the people you lead. To help you take this thinking further, I've included additional material at the end of each lesson.

Is this a workbook or a book to be read?

One of my favourite Irish sayings is "You'll never plough a field by turning it over in your mind." I'd be surprised if simply reading this book doesn't shift your thinking. At the same time, far too many books are interesting at the time but deliver precious little tangible value. You'll take more away if you invest in answering the various questions I pose throughout, whether that's on your own or in discussion with others. They're questions developed from my work as a coach and they're designed to make a real difference to the way you operate.

Additional resources

You'll find additional resources designed to help you with this book at www.leaderspace.com/TBF-resources. These include short articles on related topics that I've referenced but not had the space to address fully here, as well as printable copies of some of the pages in the book, in case you need more space to write on them or you're not keen to write in the book itself.

Do I need to read or have read 'ARC Leadership'?

No. *ARC Leadership* is a manifesto for a better class of leadership in a world that's increasingly complex and where trust is in ever-shorter supply. As such, it focuses on those three ARC Qualities (authenticity, responsibility and courage), the challenges leaders face in embodying those qualities, the tensions within and between the three qualities, and how – as leaders – we can get better at being simultaneously authentic, responsible and courageous.

The Boss Factor attends primarily to the other side of that relationship. It complements and builds on the work in my previous book but neither relies on it nor replaces it. Authenticity, responsibility and courage are the common touchpoints, with *ARC Leadership* digging deeper into those three qualities than we can here and *The Boss Factor* going broader.

What about my team?

This book focuses on upwards one-to-one relationships. I'm not ignoring the dynamics in your wider team of peers, just trying to focus our attention. I plan to cover teams in another book.

● ● ●

1

Lesson 1:
Have a vision of your own

• ● •

- Why it's not only your boss who should have a vision

- How vision drives your performance, morale and relationships with others

- Reasons not to have a vision, and why and how to overcome them

- How to generate a vision that is compelling for you and inspiring for others

SOME PEOPLE THINK their bosses should be the ones with the vision, not them. They believe – or simply assume, without thinking it through – that their seniors should be the ones with the grand plans and that they and their colleagues should just get behind the people in charge and do as they're told.

They're wrong. The chances are that – for you, like most other people – succeeding in your chosen career takes (and will continue to take) a fair degree

> "A vision is not just a picture of what could be; it is an appeal to our better selves, a call to become something more"
>
> Rosabeth Moss Kanter,[6]
> Professor at Harvard Business School

of effort. It takes commitment. It means tackling difficult situations and being resilient in the face of moral dilemmas, mistakes, failures, ambiguity and sometimes intense pressure. To maintain that resilience we all need a sense of what we're trying to achieve, where we're trying to get to in life. If we're blindly following the people that are leading us, we'll find ourselves losing our sense of perspective. We'll find it harder to see progress in our careers and broader lives. Sure, we'll be ticking off the tasks on our to-do lists, but periodically we'll feel like a rat in a spinning wheel and we'll be overly affected when our bosses move on. Having our own vision for ourselves and our careers gives us a sense of purpose and forward movement. As long as it's sufficiently flexible, your vision will carry you through times of significant change and upheaval – both at work and at home. On a purely materialistic level, research highlights a clear sense of purpose as a significant contributor to people's potential for earning and accumulating wealth, irrespective of your personality, skills and other contributing factors[7].

Whether you call it a vision or not is up to you. Some people find the word too grandiose or over-used. You might prefer the terms 'career direction', 'ambition', 'aspiration', 'mission', 'purpose' or 'true north', or a different term entirely. Whatever you call it, it's the direction you want to be heading. If that direction is out of line with the direction your boss, team and/or organisation have chosen, then you'll be at odds with them. That could be a good thing: you might be one of the people who changes that existing direction for the better. It could also be a bad thing: you could spend your time in that organisation, with that team or boss, always

feeling like you don't really fit in, like you don't buy into what you're all there to do. Feeling inauthentic in this way will make it very, very hard for you to be truly committed, which will have a negative impact on your performance, your health, your sense of fulfilment, your self-esteem and possibly even your relationships both at work and outside of work.

Having clarity on your own vision helps you be clear with others and helps you work out whether and how you can get your own needs met while meeting the needs of the team, your boss and your organisation – only then can you truly commit to the team's common objectives.

Your vision is a starting point for negotiations. It's a reason to hire you in the first place – it certainly says something about a leader if they'd value someone with a clear sense of purpose *less* than someone without.

Your vision is a lens through which to consider every challenge, dilemma and job offer that comes your way. It's a tool that'll help you decide how to lead and who to follow. It's what sits at the core of conversations with your boss about your career, the year ahead, your performance reviews, your strengths and weaknesses. It's the healthiest way to measure your own progress in life. It's far healthier than comparing yourself to others, which is guaranteed to erode one's confidence. It's far healthier than measuring our success by the size of salaries or bonuses. That's not just because our income is highly exposed to external forces, but because money quickly becomes a hygiene factor rather than a motivator. To quote someone I coached who earned around a million pounds (US$1.25 million) a year, "I can't get a job anywhere else because they won't pay me as much and I need to maintain this income to service all my debt".

Having a vision for yourself helps you be clear in your own mind regarding:

- What you want and what you need, and the difference between the two – by way of example, I may want a beer at the end of a hard day at work, but if I truly *need* one I may have a drinking problem

- The relative importance of your various wants and needs – what's critical and what's nice to have

- The various paths available that could help you meet those needs – and it's best to have several routes available.

Importantly, this is not about setting a narrow, selfish and unwavering route for ourselves with no scope for compromise, no space for others and no room for opportunism. Few people appreciate followers or team mates who come across as dogmatic and self-serving. Let's face it: we have enough of that nonsense from the small minority of narcissists and psychopaths who already exist in the workplace – but more about them later.

Why might you not have (or want) a vision?

When my friend and colleague Peter Young reviewed this chapter, he was struck by his own resistance to doing the exercises I'm about to offer you. Being a coach, he took some time to think about his resistance and was kind enough to share his insights[8]:

- "If I have a 'vision' of the future, I'll have to actually start doing things differently, change my ingrained behaviours, and in truth I really *don't* want to do that!"

- "It's very likely that in the first instance I won't know how to achieve my vision. I'll feel rather confused, which is a feeling I'd much rather avoid!"

- "If I start to think about having a different lifestyle … and then I fail to make progress towards it… well, it would surely have been better not to have thought about it in the first place!"

There are other reasons, too, to resist having a vision – beyond the fear of change, the fear of failure and the fear of responsibility (to ourselves or others). The world changes constantly: like the ocean it's never truly stable. So it's tempting to leave our lives to chance – to the pull of the current, the push of the wind, the smash of the waves – rather than attempting to decide on a destination and plot a course. Choosing a single destination also risks choosing not to pursue other paths, limiting our options. We ourselves change, so the destination we choose today might not seem so attractive further down the line. Add to that our competing priorities, the lack of time we have in our busy lives to stop and think about the future, and the fact that people in positions above and around us make many of the decisions that influence our options in life, and you've quite a few reasons not to bother having a vision.

As Peter himself said when reflecting on his own resistance, it's important to acknowledge these reasons and our animal instinct to do what's easiest. Having a vision isn't the easiest option. If it was, everyone would already have done it. It takes work – work the following questions will make a whole lot easier. And it takes belief – belief in yourself and in the fact that the mass of benefits we covered above will far outweigh the short-term downsides of creating a vision of your own.

Creating your vision

While some people relish the opportunity to pause, reflect and create a vision for the future, it's fairly common for people to feel intimidated by the whole idea. The following five-step process is tried and tested, with a range of people at different levels of seniority in a range of organisations. We'll start by widening things out, thinking 'big, deep and a long way ahead'. Then we'll get more specific. Then, in Step 3, you'll hone your vision, challenging it and running it through a reality check, to increase its chances of success. Then you'll put some concrete, practical plans and actions in place to help you make initial progress. In Step 5, you'll articulate that vision to a handful of trusted allies who can support and challenge you on the way.

Step 1: think big, think deep, think a long way ahead

Some people really struggle with the notion of thinking five years ahead, let alone fifteen. They prefer to set shorter-term goals or to avoid setting goals altogether. For some, this is because of the way they're wired. For others, it's a learned behaviour: most organisations encourage us to work at an accelerating pace and focus our attention on urgent, short-term demands. This robs us of one of the key characteristics that differentiate human beings from other animals: the ability to think ahead and plan for the future. How can we complain about short-termism in the leaders and organisations around us if we're unable to escape it ourselves?

Setting a vision that's just six months away limits our aspirations and our ability to fulfil our potential. It's the equivalent of setting off for base camp, then getting there and looking for the next logical place to go, then getting there and looking for the next waypoint, then the next... until we reach the top of the mountain, cast our eyes over the landscape around us and realise there are other mountains we'd rather be standing on top of. Unfortunately, few of us can afford a helicopter to another mountain, or have sufficient time left in our lives to scramble back down and climb another.

Looking a year ahead simply gets us to the same point in the next performance year and keeps us focused on our ratings in the next appraisal, our current projects or our case for the next promotion. Casting your mind three years into the future is more productive as there's a fair chance that by then you'll have been promoted, will have moved jobs and/or moved companies. If that's as far as you'd like to go, well then that's absolutely fine. The most distinctive contributors in organisations, though – those who are more valuable to their bosses and stakeholders, those who truly thrive – are those who are thinking bigger and aspiring to something more than mere promotions. They'll be looking five, ten, even twenty years ahead. They'll also be thinking about more than just themselves, their CVs, job titles or salaries, but more about that shortly.

You'll want to take 5-15 minutes to think about the following questions. Now might not feel like the time, but the chances are you'll never be *given* this time: you'll have to make it for yourself. At the very least book some time in your diary now to come back, answer these questions and complete the rest of the five steps in this lesson.

What 3-5 things are you really, really good at?

....

....

....

....

....

....

....

What 3-5 things have you most enjoyed in the work you've done in your career to date? What is it about those things that you have particularly enjoyed?

....

....

....

....

....

....

....

What 3-5 things have you least enjoyed? What was it about those things that you'd rather avoid in future?

....

....

....

What 3-5 things do you genuinely *need*, rather than simply *want* from your career?

....

....

....

What growth areas do you see in your organisation / profession, its offering(s) and its market over the next 3-5 years?

....

....

....

How do you see its customers', clients' or service users' needs evolving over the next 3-5 years?

....

....

....

What do you want your overall lifestyle to be like in 10-15 years' time?

....

....

....

....

What do you want your overall lifestyle (in and outside of work) to be like between now and then?

....

....

....

Step 2: write your vision down

The act of writing something down forces us to get clearer in our thinking. Where a vision is concerned, the consensus is that it's best to distil our aspirations into something simple, focused, vivid and emotive. Remember, we're looking for something that's useful as a guide to future decision-making, something you can call to mind quickly and decisively. The more complex or vague it is, the less memorable it will be. Some of the people I've worked with have made the mistake of thinking that making it emotive is overly sentimental or faddish. For them, it conjures images of cheerleaders, or pumped up salespeople or executives pounding their chests and shouting "rah". That's not what I'm talking about here. If it's going to motivate you and help you navigate complexity, distractions and temptations, your vision needs to mean something to you. What I'm really talking about is the basic science of motivation: if your vision triggers no emotional reaction at all, it's meaningless and you'll ditch it at the first sign of trouble. You'll probably even have forgotten it by the time you've finished this book.

Really important here is that you get beyond the short term. Statements like "I want to have built an IT department with five times as many people as it has now" are far too grounded in what you're currently doing. That's an objective, not a vision. Visions are more abstract, more qualitative than quantitative, and are rooted in something deeper within us, something we're really passionate about. They're generally something a child would understand. For example, a vision that might lead to someone building that IT bigger department might be something like "I want to transform the way IT brings value to organisations, so when people think of us they see us as allies and enablers".

So, write a single emotive, focused and descriptive sentence that sums up what you want your work and broader life to look and feel like in 10-15 years' time.

Now, to give yourself a real, clear and tangible sense of what that means and will look like, write a paragraph or 3-5 bullet points of further detail, fleshing out that single sentence.

....

....

....

....

....

....

....

Step 3: hone your vision

To make it sufficiently useful and robust, we'll need to test and hone that vision. So, try asking yourself these questions:

How bold is your vision? Is it over-ambitious? Could it be bolder, and if so how?

....

....

....

....

....

If the things you do well were written in one circle and the things you enjoy were written in another, how well does your vision target the overlap between those two circles?

How well does it factor in your aspirations for your life outside work, your family, the people around you at work...?

What are the potential downsides for you and/or others in the pursuit or success of this vision?

What will you need to give up to achieve it?

....

....

....

Now re-write your vision taking your answers into account:

....

....

....

....

Step 4: prepare your vision for the road ahead

Turning this vision into reality will take effort, potentially rather a lot of it, and there'll inevitably be challenges along the way. The following questions are designed to help you overcome those challenges.

Whose commitment will you need in order to make this happen?
It's best to include people inside and outside of your organisation and to consider what commitment you'll need from people in your personal life, e.g. your family, partner / spouse, friends. Given the timeframe we're talking about, in some cases you'll be better keeping things more general – for instance, 'my boss' rather than 'Michelle'.

....

....

....

What knowledge, experience and skills will you need to have / develop in yourself if you are going to make this vision a reality?

....

....

....

....

....

What are the 3-5 trickiest obstacles you'll face and how will you overcome them?

	Obstacle	How I'll overcome it
1		
2		
3		
4		
5		

Step 5: tell someone about it

One of the most effective ways to motivate ourselves and open up opportunities to achieve our aspirations is to make sure other people know about what we're trying to achieve. Pick three people from different areas of your life, including your work life, and share your vision with them. You might seek input or feedback. You might just want them to listen and take it in. In my experience, it's best to make it clear in advance which of those things you're looking for. There are times when I've wanted someone's advice or coaching on my chosen course of action and there are times when all I've really wanted was an encouraging nod.

Write the names of those three people here, then tick them off once you've spoken to them:

Name   **Feedback (if any)**

Applying this lesson as a leader of others

If you're a leader in your own right, you might already be thinking of ways to use this lesson with the people you lead. The first consideration, really, is how well you're role-modelling having a vision. Do the people you lead know your aspirations? To reference the underlying framework for this book (see right), how authentic does that vision seem to them? What do your actions day-by-day say about your commitment to that vision? How courageously do they see you pursuing the direction

you've chosen in the face of obstacles or distractions? In what ways do you show responsibility in relation to that vision by taking into account others' needs and perspectives, rather than blindly or zealously pursuing your own agenda?

Then there's the question of alignment. It's pretty clear from my work developing high-performing teams that team members and their leaders find it very difficult to fully commit to a shared direction and put the team's collective results ahead of their own if that shared direction isn't sufficiently aligned with the individual directions each of them wants to take. All too often:

- The team and its leader fail to recognise this

- People pretend they're willing to sacrifice their own desires, needs and agendas but subsequently demonstrate quite clearly that they aren't

- People avoid telling their colleagues about any needs, desires or agendas they think won't be taken seriously, might cause conflict or that they find embarrassing.

This lack of awareness and openness creates an illusion of alignment that risks undermining everyone's commitment, success, willingness to collaborate and their enjoyment of the work. So, how clear is it to the people you lead that your vision is aligned to the direction the organisation needs to head if it's to meet the needs and aspirations of its people and its stakeholders? To what extent can the people you lead align their own visions behind yours and thus fully commit to the direction you've chosen? To what extent do they see fulfilling your vision as a means to meet their own needs and aspirations, versus purely serving yours?

Finally, there's the question of the extent to which you help your people formulate, articulate and achieve their own visions. Are you an enabler and/or ally in that regard? Or are you a bystander, or even an obstacle?

All of these questions work as a standalone, but they also dovetail well with the conversations you might want to have with the people you lead once you've tackled Lesson 2.

In summary

It's easy to write off 'having a vision' as fluff or something the people above us should do. However, a sense of our own direction helps increase our motivation, resilience and satisfaction with our jobs and lives in general. It gives us our 'true north', guiding us through difficult times and decisions, and offers a better, healthier way of measuring progress than the alternative benchmarks available to us. There are challenges when it comes to creating a vision, but this lesson has given you tools to overcome those challenges. If you've used them you'll have a clear, compelling statement of intent that's been thoroughly tested and backed up with clear actions to get you started. You'll also have identified some potential allies who can help you hone your vision and turn it into reality.

• ● •

Lesson 2:
Choose your leader wisely

• What do you need in a boss if you're truly going to thrive?

- How much choice do you REALLY have?

- What do you need in a boss if you're truly going to thrive?

- What factors can and can't you influence?

- How to evaluate the potential for a successful relationship

OF ALL THE LESSONS

in this book, this is the one to which people have had the strongest knee-jerk reactions. I understand why: many people believe they've no choice over who gets to be their boss – or, at least, that their choices are very, very limited. Some feel trapped in their current roles, working for bosses they really don't like, who stifle their creativity and offer them little or no autonomy while piling on the pressure day after day.

You might be one of those people, or you might be someone who's had to choose between a number of options at several points in your life. Either way,

> "After all is said and done, you are free to choose but you are not free from the consequence of your choice"

Original source unknown[9]

while I know the title of this lesson is contentious, my intention is to help you spot the choices you do have and to leverage those choices to create opportunities to improve things. Improving things might mean making a bad situation better or turning a good relationship with your boss into one that's truly distinctive and creates additional value for you, for them and the people around you.

To show you what I mean, I'd like you to take a moment to think about the best boss you've ever had. Consider the things they did and the qualities they had that cause you to remember them as such a good boss.

Then think about the choices you made in life and your career that brought the two of you together, and the things you did at the beginning of that relationship that set that relationship up for success.

Now think of the boss you found most challenging, who contributed least positively to your life, job satisfaction, performance in the role and to your career in general. Again, remind yourself of the things they did and the qualities they had or lacked.

Then consider the life and career choices you made that led to you being in that particular role in that particular organisation at that exact time, which meant you had them as your boss. Think about the weeks just before they became your boss and the things you did, the questions you asked, the people you consulted, the way you prepared ahead of time. Then consider the things you could, perhaps, have done differently in the early days of that relationship that might have increased its chances of success.

Looking at each of those two bosses, what 'due diligence' did you do before the relationship began? Did you go into that relationship with your eyes wide open or did you enter it blindly? Did you enter that 'marriage' knowing little about the person you were marrying? Or maybe you were ignorant but characteristically optimistic? Were you disappointed with their flaws but convinced you could change them? Or begrudgingly resigned to their imperfections and a life of rolling your eyes and tutting? Or did you begin that relationship with a robust assessment of their strengths, style and manageable limitations that confirmed your gut instinct that this would be a truly successful and enjoyable relationship?

The chances are you're like most people. When looking at the amount of research people do when preparing to join a new organisation, The Institute of Leadership and Management (ILM) found that 28% of people put in less than an hour's research and 42% spend 1-4 hours; 6% really go to town and put in more than 12 hours[10]. The focus of that research, though, seems to be on the organisation – its strategy, its reputation and so on.

The ILM's report makes no mention of people endeavouring to find out more about their boss. The fact that most of the data people are collecting comes from the organisation itself and the internet suggests most people really are lacking boss-specific insights into what it'll take to make that new relationship a success. It's little surprise, then, that only 68% of new starters found clear connections between the information provided in advance and the actual work. I wonder how closely the remaining 32% match the 30% of new joiners (see below) who're already intending to leave within their first 12 months, with two thirds of those actively looking right now?

Revolving doors

- 30% of new starters plan to leave their job within the first 12 months[11]
- 19% are currently actively looking for a new role[12]
- 40% of people who leave voluntarily do so in the first 6 months[13]
- Across the research, the most commonly cited reason for people leaving an organisation is their boss[14]

My point here is that you are not *to blame* for your boss's shortcomings, any more than you can take credit for their strengths, but the vast majority of the factors that determine whether our bosses succeed or fail lie in the *relationships* they have with the people around them – their

. other senior stakeholders, their peers, the people they
. the people they live with whom we and their other colleagues
ᴊnt never see or hear about. Likewise, the success or failure of you
relationship with any given boss rests in the *relationship* you have with
them, and both of you play your parts in that relationship. Both of you
bring good things and bad things to it. Both of you make choices about
how – and whether – to be with each other. So both of you need to take
responsibility for those choices and for their consequences, even if one
of you is 90% 'to blame' and the other only 10%.

All choices are made within constraints. Some constraints are tighter
than others and different people have different reactions to different
constraints. In most cases, for instance, when we apply for a job the
leader is already in position. Similarly, when our existing leader leaves,
it's usually their seniors who choose their replacement. In addition, many
people work in matrix management structures or work in project teams
where they move from project to project (and leader to leader) every few
weeks or months.

In all of these situations, even when we're feeling the pressure of
various constraints, we always have a choice. We might be sitting in an
interview thinking "This person seems like a nightmare to work with", as I'm
sure we've all done at some point. We could have a bad feeling about our
old boss's replacement or of the person being lined up to be in charge of
our next project. In each case, I believe we have four options available:

- Choose a different job in a different team or organisation, where
  we'll have the chance to follow a better leader – after all, a wealth of
  research strongly suggests that the primary reason for any individual
  choosing to quit their job is their relationship with their boss

- Replace the leader for another leader – I was once on an exec team
  that passed a very public vote of no confidence in the organisation's
  president. It was distinctly unpleasant and, I felt, unfair on this
  occasion, but it's always an option

- Find a way to change the leader's behaviour by challenging their current ways of working and thinking and/or encouraging them to adopt a different approach; Lessons 5, 6 and 9 in particular can help with this

- Challenge ourselves to adapt our own behaviours and/or mind-set to get the best from the situation – there are far fewer perfect bosses than truly terrible ones; sometimes it's how we think about and work with our existing boss that makes the biggest difference.

Okay, I have a choice, however hard it might be. So what should I look for?

I consider myself very, very lucky to have had some really good bosses in my time. With the benefit of hindsight, I can see that those bosses who had the greatest impact on my life and career weren't all great *leaders* in a wider sense, but they had some critical attributes that enabled them to get the best from me as a follower and as a leader in my own right.

So what makes me say they were great bosses but not necessarily great leaders? It was the fact that they delivered on some but not all of those Three Core Disciplines and three ARC Qualities so critical in the relationship between a leader and the people they lead and serve.

I'd say everyone I think of as a good boss was Authentic. They all also did a good job of securing my commitment and building my capacity. Some weren't as Courageous as they could have been. Others could have had been clearer, more informed or more decisive in their direction. Some could have been more inspiring by creating a mission for the team or organisation that required us to be more collectively Responsible for something more meaningful to us all and that would have made a bigger difference in the world beyond our walls.

The net result was that their approach to leading benefited me and many of my colleagues, but these bosses didn't all deliver on their own potential or that of our departments or organisations. I'm not being ungrateful when I say that: these are people who have shaped me as a person; people who, early in my career, took a leap of faith in employing me when on paper I wouldn't have seemed the best candidate for the job. They're people who gave me the tricky blend of autonomy, challenge and support that it takes to keep me keen and get the best out of me. If I could re-run the last thirty years of my life, it would be a pleasure and an honour to have that time with them again. I'd also like to think I'd do a better job of helping them to deliver on those Three Core Disciplines and three ARC qualities, by learning from these ten lessons and taking greater responsibility for their ability to deliver.

The focus right now, though, is on looking for the right leader for *you*. Some readers have asked for a checklist to help them do their due diligence – a list of questions to ask at interview and/or when researching a potential new boss. So we're building that into the work we do face to face with people who're looking for better relationships with their bosses. The most important thing, though, is that you decide for yourself the kind of leader you want to work with. So let's start with four key criteria that will determine whether someone is the best boss for you:

1. The extent to which following them will help you thrive

2. The extent to which their leadership will have a positive impact on the rest of their team and the organisation as a whole

3. The extent to which their mission will have a positive, lasting impact on the world beyond the organisation

4. The extent to which the environment in which that leader works will enable you to thrive.

It's easy to be lured in and distracted by Number 1. It's an important piece of the puzzle, but if your chosen leader fails on the other three criteria, you'll reap a far smaller return on the time and energy you're investing in following them. You'll be risking adopting a mind-set that is overly narrow, self-centred and immature, and risking earning the kind of reputation that mind-set deserves. Then you'll carry that reputation into your next role and the next, limiting your ability to fulfil your own potential in that organisation and others. So let's start with Number 1 but pay due attention to criteria 2, 3 and 4.

Choice Factor 1: your boss's potential to help you thrive

You might be seeking some very tangible benefits from the relationship with your boss: the prestige of working with them if they're well respected; access to their networks; learning from their technical expertise; opportunities to be their successor when they move up the hierarchy, take a job elsewhere or retire. There might be other factors they could bring to the relationship that'll help you thrive. Similarly, there will be external sources of motivation that engage you, like praise, money, status, performance ratings and the approval of others, as well as the more intrinsic motivational factors like doing things because you enjoy them or find them interesting.

You've a wealth of experiences behind you that'll help you identify what leaders need to do to motivate you and to create the conditions for you to thrive. To make good use of those experiences, I recommend using the graph overleaf to draw your lifeline from childhood to the present day. The horizontal axis is 'Time': to the far right is today, to the far left is the day you were born. The vertical axis shows the extent to which you were thriving at that point in your life. A score of ten means you were fully committed and enthused, 'in the zone', performing well and growing as a person and/or professional. A score of zero means you were barely surviving. Be sure to label each event or period in your life in a way that's meaningful to you, as you'll be coming back to this graph shortly and may want to return to it in future. Pay particular attention to writing in the names of the bosses or other leadership figures (including parents and grandparents, where appropriate) who played a key role in your life at the time.

Please note: people put different meanings on the word 'surviving', but the focus here is on the realm of motivation, emotion and your psychological sense of growth, progress and/or well-being. I know a number of people who have survived in war zones; some of those were civilians who would rate the experience as a zero on this scale and some were professional soldiers, who wouldn't say they enjoyed the experience per se, but would rate it highly as a time when they were highly motivated, felt well-equipped to handle the pressure and were developing their capacity to deal with that kind of environment. After all, it's often the hardships in our lives that are the catalysts for the greatest growth. So, however you define 'surviving' and 'thriving', be sure to be consistent in your application of those definitions. They're definitions you can live by and use as benchmarks in the future.

TIME

FROM SURVIVING TO TRULY THRIVING

10   0

When you've completed your lifeline, review it and answer the following questions:

What were the 3-5 key factors that contributed to you thriving, rather than simply surviving (or even struggling)?

....

....

....

....

....

....

Bearing those key factors in mind, what 3-5 things will you need in your relationship with your boss if that relationship is to help you thrive?

....

....

....

....

....

....

....

....

....

What 3-5 things will you need to avoid, limit or manage in the relationship with your boss if you want to reduce the chances of encountering or creating conditions that will make it *harder* for you to thrive?

....

....

....

....

....

Choice Factor 2: your boss's potential impact on his / her team and organisation

Most successful people know that their success has depended on more than their own qualities and efforts, and those of the people who've led and mentored them. They recognise the role played by the teams in which they've worked. You may have met people who seemed to be relying on their peers underperforming to make them look good. It's easy to judge them as lazy, incompetent or spiteful, but they could instead be demotivated or insecure, perhaps because of poor leadership or some other mistreatment or bad luck in the past. Whatever the causes, though, the best people – whether they're following or leading or both – thrive in environments where their whole team is succeeding. The reasons are fairly consistent across organisations and cultures. For instance:

- A certain amount of *healthy* competition motivates us to try harder and seek out new challenges. Healthy competition is undertaken consciously and responsibly, with the focus on better outcomes for the team's stakeholders rather than on promoting the competitors' self-interest. So in the pursuit of healthy competition, it's worth asking "What are we competing over?" and "For whose benefit are we competing?"

- Enthusiasm and energy are contagious, and when we're more enthused and energised most of us are:

  - More motivated

  - More creative

  - More able to see the bigger picture

  - Less likely to succumb to our own counter-productive stress behaviours

- Increasingly, we rely on others to feed us information, help us identify problems and potential solutions and to get things done – none of which they're likely to do if they're preoccupied with surviving in a toxic, stodgy or uninspiring environment.

So it's worth assessing the extent to which your leader helps create an environment where your team members (or prospective team members) thrive. I say 'helps' because no leader can do this on their own. Their ability to create that environment will be affected by the organisation's culture and the actions of their other followers. It will also be affected by the actions of other leaders and teams whose work or sphere of influence overlaps with theirs. At the same time, the leader's behaviour will have a disproportionate impact on the culture of the team and on the extent to which that team culture enhances of reduces people's motivation, performance and professional growth.

You'll have your own thoughts regarding what helps people thrive, including the factors that will have emerged if you completed the lifeline graph a couple of pages ago. Here are some factors others have come up with. I've used their words and resisted the urge to remove any apparent contradictions or factors that can be disastrous if overplayed.

- Allows us creative freedom

- Has the support of the team's key stakeholders

- Ensures we have the processes and resources in place to achieve our goals

- Facilitates our growth in our chosen directions

- Encourages us to think big

- Allows us to make mistakes

- Puts the right people with the right talent in the right places

- Is our biggest supporter (individually and collectively), showing respect and faith in us and our abilities

- Is more focused on the team's success than their own personal glory

- Doesn't tell us "You can't…"

- Helps us be realistic about life's ups and downs

- Offers clarity

- Gives me advice on anything but not everything

- When I'm definitely lost, tells me what to do

- Shares their wisdom, without assuming it *is* wisdom

- Enables me to make the right decisions for the time and context.

The extent to which your boss displays each of those behaviours will affect the extent to which he or she creates the conditions for you and the rest of their people to thrive. As we'll see in subsequent lessons, your boss's ability to do so will be influenced by a number of things: their leadership mind-set, established habits and changing needs; the demands placed on them by their various stakeholders; and their relationships with you and other people they lead. Where their relationship with you is concerned, each of the lessons in this book helps you to help them create the conditions that will enable you and your colleagues to thrive. We'll focus for now on how a leader's patterns of behaviour can undermine their ability to create the conditions in which their people will thrive.

In Lesson 1, we acknowledged the existence of leaders who are boring and self-centred. The reality is, we all have our weaknesses and none of us has a style of working or leading that will appeal to everyone. Nevertheless, it's worth watching out for some common behaviours that may reduce the probability that you and your team mates will thrive under a given leader. These are often the result of a leader overplaying genuine strengths or applying behaviours that were successful in one context but are no longer appropriate. It's easy to judge people who display these tendencies, but it's far more helpful to try to *understand* what's causing them.

Far and away my favourite tool for assessing leaders' risk of 'derailing' themselves and/or the people they lead is Hogan's Development Survey, otherwise known as The Dark Side[15]. The following checklist is based very much on Hogan's work and the work of one of his competitors[16], with the language tweaked to reflect the focus of this current lesson. As you read through the list, I'd encourage you to tick those you recognise in your boss(es), but also to notice which apply to you.

- *Butterfly enthusiasm:* when a boss presents a big new idea or initiative with a burst of enthusiasm then gets distracted by their desire to find the 'next big thing' and struggles to finish what they've started or support their people in doing so on their behalf

- *Over-confidence:* which risks being seen as arrogance and can cause leaders to be over-bearing and even intimidating, refusing to listen to others' opinions – either because they're convinced their own opinion is right, they're afraid to be wrong or they're actually overcompensating for feelings of inadequacy

- *Exploitation:* when the ability to charm, influence and get the best out of people is overplayed and becomes overly self-serving

- *Recklessness:* when their appetite for success, respect and/or risk crosses the line from 'courageous' to 'irresponsible', with the probability and benefits of winning outweighed by the probability and potential cost of failure, or success coming at too high a price

- *Unbridled eccentricity:* when interesting quirks evolve into self-centred inflexibility, superficial exuberance and/or a lack of clarity, consistency, pragmatism or rigour in their decisions and actions

- *Difficulty trusting others:* when political astuteness and an ability to read their stakeholders is overplayed and leads to cynical mistrust of others' motives, which often then develops into a tendency to place the blame on anyone but oneself

- *Excessive risk avoidance*: when the desire to get things right stifles innovation and proactivity and potentially causes the leader to avoid situations that might require them to assert themselves and their authority

- *Interpersonal detachment:* when a leader's natural independence and task-focus causes them to overlook the need to empathise or sees them drift away entirely, opening them up to charges of being cold-hearted, and isolated, maybe even causing feelings of isolation in others

- *Passive aggression:* when a focused, structured approach combines with a fear of open conflict and causes a leader to resent the people they feel are making life difficult; in the worst cases this leads to bitching, back-stabbing and workplace sabotage

- *Perfectionism:* which can stifle effective delegation and risks undermining your confidence, morale and opportunities to grow

- *Upwards dependency:* when your boss is so concerned about what their superiors think of them that they'll find it hard to stand up for you and the rest of the team.

Some of the research suggests the 'dark side' traits at the top half of the list are more common in the private sector and those in the bottom half are more common in the public sector[17]. Some studies suggest certain traits are more common in certain types of role (perfectionism in finance and recklessness in sales, for example[18]). Other research has found some derailers to be more common for one gender than another (exploitation, recklessness and interpersonal detachment being a little more common in male leaders than female, for instance, and risk avoidance and eagerness to please being a little more common in women[19]).

> We'll return to these potential derailers but if – at the end of this book – you're still keen for more depth and detail, I'd highly recommend taking a look at the book *Why CEOs Fail*[20]

Personally, though, I'm wary of stereotyping. I believe it's simply important to remember that most of us will demonstrate one or more of these bad habits at times – particularly under stress – and that each of them is the downside of a genuine strength. After all, having high standards and attention to detail is an important virtue in many situations; it's only when it becomes counter-productive perfectionism that we have a problem. When assessing your potential leader's likely impact on you and the rest of their team, what you need to work out is how frequently and extremely he or she displays these negative behaviours.

Choice Factor 3: your boss's potential impact on the world beyond their organisation

There's a lot of talk about how the young generation is more focused than previous generations on the contribution their work and their organisations make to the world around them. Personally, I hate the idea of ascribing single, simplistic traits to whole generations – whether they're Millennials, Baby Boomers, Gen X, Gen Y or Z. Yes, the world has changed in many, many ways since the Gen X folk were in their formative years. In the UK, for instance, some people born in the 1960s were able to buy a house at the age of 22 with no help from their parents, which is far less likely now. Similarly, we no longer have final salary pension plans and the term 'job for life' is taking on a very different meaning – less the reassurance that many people felt in the latter half of the Twentieth Century that they would stay in the same organisation for their entire working life, more the realisation that many of us will retire far later in life than our parents and grandparents.

Historically, though, most 13-25 year olds have been branded by their parents' generation as idealistic or impatient upstarts with no respect for the status quo. I also know many retirees who are doing far more for society than most teenagers or recent graduates. The reality is: many of us want to feel that our work makes a difference to the world[21]. Our wider contribution is almost always cited as the pinnacle of moral and personal development, and the most advanced leadership mind-set. After all, there are ethical *and* commercial arguments to think of beyond our own, individual daily needs. So, if you're that way inclined, you'd be wise to consider your leader's current and potential impact on the world outside the organisation. Are they likely to do more harm than good, more good than harm, or pretty much balance the scales? And your assessment (and the importance you place on this choice factor) should guide your decisions regarding whether and how to work with them. One thing is well worth remembering, though, as you reflect on how much this choice factor means to you: if a leader doesn't care about the world beyond their organisation there's a higher probability that they won't really care about you either.

Choice Factor 4: the extent to which your boss's environment will enable you to thrive

Like our own, any boss's behaviour is largely determined by four things: their needs, their ways of seeing the world, the habits they've formed over the course of their lives, and the environment in which they operate.

We tend to massively underestimate the influence of the environment on others and overestimate the extent to which their behaviour is driven by forces within them. It's only fairly rarely that we get to have the same boss in a completely different organisation, so it's hard for us to see that the great bosses of our past may have seemed shockingly awful if they'd been our boss somewhere else. Likewise, those bosses whose apparent dreadfulness has earned them a place in our hearts for all the wrong reasons might have been real assets to us under different circumstances.

The right leader for you will need to be working in the right environment for you. Any leader who isn't will find it very difficult to deliver on your needs and expectations. So ask yourself:

What kind of organisation do I need to work for* if I'm going to thrive? *(If you completed the lifeline graph under Choice Factor 1, then that will have provided some insights here. I'd also recommend considering the culture, structure and purpose of the organisation, as well as the kind of market in which it operates.)*

....

....

....

....

What do I notice in this organisation that motivates me and enables me to thrive?

....

....

....

---

*   If you're working in more of a freelance capacity and/or across multiple organisations, then it's worth replacing the word "for" with the word "with" when answering this question.

What is it about the organisation that detracts (or could detract) from my ability to thrive, or make it harder for my boss to help me thrive? And what actions can I take to respond to that?

....

....

....

Your current or future boss

How does your current boss – or the boss you're currently considering working with – rate on each of the four 'Choice Factors' we've covered? *(If you don't have a boss at the moment, you may find it useful to rate your most recent boss, to help you assess what it is you'll need in your next boss.)*

	Obstacle	Score (0-10)
1	The extent to which following them motivates and benefits you	
2	The extent to which their leadership has a positive impact on the rest of their team and the organisation as a whole	
3	The extent to which their 'mission' has a positive, lasting impact on the world beyond the organisation	
4	The extent to which their environment enables them to create the conditions in which you'll thrive	

If you've put real thought into the ratings you've given above, the work you've done here will offer you greater clarity as to whether the boss you're looking at is the right boss for you. What you do with that clarity is up to you. Whatever your decision, you'll find the other lessons in this book will help you put it into action.

Applying this lesson as a leader of others

If you're a leader in your own right, you're probably already wondering about your people's right to choose whether to be led by you and how you'd measure up against the four key criteria at the heart of this lesson. You might have even have read that list of potential 'dark side' derailers on page 48 and recognised some in yourself.

I'd encourage you to take some time to answer the question "Why would anyone want to be led by me?" In doing so, I'd recommend assessing yourself against criteria 2, 3 and 4 in the table above. If you really want to dig deep, you might even ask a few trusted people to tell you which of those dark side derailers they think can sometimes apply to you. We'll revisit them in other lessons, but the option is also there to take Hogan's actual assessment[22].

Depending on your existing relationships with them, it could then be well worth engaging each of your staff in a conversation around that first criterion: the extent to which following you motivates and benefits them and creates the conditions in which they, personally, can thrive. You might choose to do some reflection on your own before speaking to them, focusing on each team member in turn, or you might begin with a conversation. You might also weave this together with any thinking you've done in response to Lesson 1, where we looked at the importance of the people you lead having visions of their own.

The choice, as always, is yours.

In summary

The idea that we can choose our leader is contentious for some. However, what I've asked you to consider is the choices you have and the choices you make. We looked at those that bring you and your boss together in the first place, those that set the frame at the start of the relationship and those that you continue to make daily in what is, after all, one of the most important working relationships you'll have at that point in time. We then looked at four key criteria for assessing the value of that relationship to you:

1. The extent to which following them will help you thrive

2. The extent to which their leadership will have a positive impact on the rest of their team and the organisation

3. The extent to which their 'mission' will have a positive, lasting impact beyond the organisation

4. The extent to which the environment in which that leader works will enable you to thrive.

These are criteria you can use when evaluating a potential new boss or senior stakeholder, or when considering the value of a relationship you're already in. If you've answered the questions I've posed, you'll have a clear picture of the kind of leader you're looking for and the extent to which those above and around you at the moment are the right leaders for you.

In the next lesson, we'll be looking at your assumptions about the nature of leadership and your experiences of the people who have led you in the past. Why? Because these affect your current and future bosses' ability to live up to your expectations and you may be setting them up to fail.

● ● ●

Lesson 3:
Challenge your assumptions

- How your assumptions and expectations might be guaranteeing disappointment in this boss and others

- What baggage are you bringing from prior relationships?

- What patterns are you repeating time and again?

- How to switch to a mind-set that's a better foundation for a successful relationship

BEFORE WE GET STARTED, I ask that you complete the following sentence

as it'll inform your thinking throughout this lesson. You can use as many words or bullet points as you like, but be authentic. Don't regurgitate what you've been told: write down what you truly believe, even if you feel uncomfortable writing it.

A good leader...

We'll come back to that sentence shortly.

I wonder if you, like me, have fallen foul of the following affliction at some point in your life? When I was in my teens and early twenties, I had this vision of the perfect woman who perhaps one day I'd meet and spend the rest of my life with. I realise now that, consciously or unconsciously, I judged each of my girlfriends against that ideal. This unattainable expectation on my part created a whole host of problems and made me less tolerant of their imperfections – many of which were the things that attracted me to them in the first place. It meant I was more inclined to see the grass as greener when I looked at my friends' relationships or considered being single again or dating someone else.

> ## The data says[23]...
>
> - The likelihood that your boss will fail is somewhere between 30 and 67 percent
> - Averaging the predictions of 12 published studies, the base probability is 47%
> - That's a *really* tough gig
> - In what ways are your expectations adding to that pressure?

Perhaps worst of all, my delusion that there was some perfect woman out there – better than the one I was with – distracted me from my own failings and unhelpful contributions to existing relationships.

Perhaps, like me, you see the same delusion playing out when it comes to your own and others' expectations of their leaders. All too often, a leader's direct reports consciously or unconsciously assume that there's some perfect leader out there – or at least an absolutely fantastic one. So they consciously or unconsciously exaggerate the flaws of their current leader, using him or her as a scapegoat, projecting their 'dark sides' onto the leader so they can avoid confronting their own failings. Some are even able to work for a succession of 'bad' bosses without considering the possibility that the problem might not be the bosses at all: it could be themselves.

The assumptions and expectations you bring to relationships with the people above you will have a huge impact on your experience of those relationships, on the ability of those people to meet your expectations and on their ability to do their jobs. Those assumptions and expectations are key ingredients in the mind-set with which you enter these relationships. They affect how you interpret your bosses' environment, role and actions. They influence the judgements you make as to their suitability, competence, character and integrity and, perhaps, even their worth as human beings. Our mind-sets shape what we attend to when others talk about our bosses and they contribute to the justifications we make for our own less-than-helpful behaviours in those relationships. So, because the mind-set you bring is *so* influential, we're going to step back from you for a moment and examine that mind-set from the outside, to get as objective a view on it as possible. Be aware, though, that your mind-set will even influence the approach you take to this lesson!

Mind-sets are complex things. Each of us is unique and my approach to this topic is continually evolving as I learn new things and my own mind-set shifts. For the purposes of this lesson, though, it's helpful to look at your mind-set through three complementary lenses:

- Relationships – what are your assumptions, expectations and beliefs regarding your interactions with other people?

- Tasks – what do you believe your and your boss's purposes are? What are you here to do?

- Agency – how do you expect the world to treat you, and to what extent do you believe you (and your boss) can adapt to and influence the world around you?

Your mind-set regarding the relationship between you and your boss

As we look at five types (or flavours) of relationship mind-set[24], I suggest you have two to three of your most significant senior stakeholders in mind, including your immediate boss. You can include a past boss, too, if you need to or it helps to do so, but do choose at least two relationships. Afterwards, I'm going to ask you to consider the extent to which each of these five flavours is reflected in the beliefs, assumptions, expectations and behaviours you bring to those relationships.

- **Compliant, dependent or accommodating:** you do what the boss says. Maybe you disagree silently in your own mind; maybe you don't. Maybe you're seeking their approval; maybe you're afraid of them and trying to stay out of trouble; maybe you like them or you think they're a genius. Maybe your confidence is low at the moment, or you're out of your depth, or short on some critical knowledge or data, or perhaps you've always felt like a bit of an impostor.

- **Defiant, counter-dependent or competing:** you work against them, perhaps in small ways, perhaps in very noticeable ways. It's irrelevant at this point whether you feel justified in doing so. What's relevant is whether, in your head, this senior figure is the opposition. You might be the hero, trying to save everyone else from this person's incompetence, short-sightedness, recklessness or bullying behaviour. You could be the rebel, the innovator or the subject matter expert, convinced your approach is in the best interests of the organisation, its clients, customers, service users, suppliers or shareholders. You could be exerting some kind of authority over them, seeking to control their behaviours – perhaps even in a well-intentioned attempt to rescue them from themselves or others. Maybe you're competing with this person for promotion or the attention of key stakeholders, or you're caught up in politicking and feel they're an obstacle or an enemy.

- **Self-reliant, independent or avoiding:** you prefer to do your own thing, working independently and following your own agenda. You're not opposed to this senior figure. You just don't need them, either because they're not highly relevant, not particularly helpful or not especially necessary. Maybe they feel the same way – about themselves, or about you. Maybe they just trust you to get on with the job.

- *Transactional, co-dependent or compromising:* you operate as if you believe each of you needs to give something in order to get some of the things they want, but that neither party should have full sway. Perhaps every request from them meets a demand or counter-request from you. Perhaps it's subtler or more amicable than that, but there's definitely a sense of give and take.

- *Alliant, interdependent or collaborating:* you genuinely want to work together with this senior person, understanding each other's needs and finding clever ways to ensure everybody gets what they need. In Sabina Spencer's words, you truly believe "If anybody loses, nobody wins."

Thinking of the two to three relationships you've had in mind as you've read through these five descriptions, turn the three circles below into pie charts indicating the extent to which you bring each of these five 'flavours' to that relationship. Here's an example to show you what I mean.

Example: me with Gemma

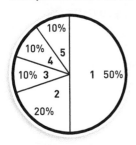

1: Compliant, dependent or accomodating
2: Defiant, counter-dependent or competing
3: Self-reliant, independent or avoiding
4: Transactional, co-dependent or compromising
5: Alliant, interdependent or collaborating

Be really, really honest here. Would these people pick the same mind-set to describe your approach to the relationship with them? My experience and the research data suggest that very few people genuinely spend most of their time operating from that fifth, collaborative mind-set, particularly in their relationships with people who have more power than them. Stepping back from the five flavours, most of us can see that the fifth is the most mature, impactful and sustainable kind of relationship. It's just that sometimes the world around, within or between us nudges us into one of the other four ways of working.

Relationship 1:   **Relationship 2:**   **Relationship 3:**

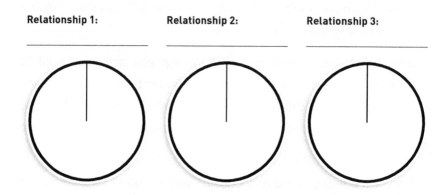

Each of those pie charts reflects the unique blend of 'flavours' you bring to those relationships when it comes to your beliefs, assumptions, expectations and behaviours. It's well worth reflecting on the following questions, to help you assess the impact of your relationship mind-set and potentially identify ways to enhance the impact you're having.

What do you notice when you compare your two / three pie charts and the mind-sets they represent?

How might your boss be interpreting the behaviours that result from your current mind-set? How might those interpretations affect the way they think of you and interact with you?

....

....

....

....

We'll come back to the actions you might take in response to these insights at the end of this lesson. Right now, I'd encourage you to take a look at the responses you gave at the start of this lesson when I asked you to complete the sentence "A good leader...". Then answer the questions below, bearing in mind that some of those responses will relate to the 'task' and 'agency' mind-sets we'll look at shortly.

What do your responses say about your general, prevailing mind-set when it comes to relationships with bosses and other senior figures? *(If you're struggling, it can help to think more generally about which of the five flavours above are most dominant in your relationship mind-set with regard to the people who lead you.)*

....

....

....

....

How did you develop that mind-set? *(e.g. What events, experiences and relationships helped form the attitudes, beliefs and habits that make up that way of operating? In what ways did your relationships with your parents, grandparents and school-teachers contribute to that mind-set?)*

....

....

....

If there are differences between that prevailing mind-set and the ones in your pie charts above, what's causing that?

....

....

....

....

If you've answered all of the questions I've posed, you might want to take a short break to let your thinking percolate for a moment before we take a look at your task mind-set. If you're reading this quickly and not currently stopping to reflect and complete the questions, then by all means keep going.

Your 'task' mind-set regarding what your boss is there to do

Having considered your mind-set with regard to the relationship you have with your boss, it's important to consider what you expect them to be doing in their role – your attitudes, beliefs, assumptions and expectations on the 'task' front. Again, if your expectations and their actions are misaligned, it'll likely be a source of friction in the relationship.

Where our mind-set around the tasks and responsibilities of a leader are concerned, I find it helpful to think in terms of seven areas[25]. Most people gravitate to one or two, some to three or four, but it's highly unlikely that a single individual will prioritise all seven equally. In the table on the following pages, you're going to identify the areas of focus for your ideal boss, yourself and your current boss. Then we'll be able to see what you're hoping for in a leader and where those expectations came from, what you think your role is and the extent to which your current boss is meeting your expectations. We'll have some insight into their likely mind-set and how the similarities and differences between yours and theirs is helping and hindering your ability to do good work – both together and apart.

For each column in the table, you have a total of ten points to distribute across each of the seven areas to reflect that person's relative focus on each of those potential priorities. I've left an eighth, empty row as there may be other things you want to include that you can't align with any of the seven areas listed.

Each column has its nuances, so I'd recommend attending to the following:

- *Ideal boss:* you've already done some work on this, when you completed that sentence at the start of this lesson, back on page 57 ("A good leader..."), so I'd strongly suggest you re-read your responses then use that as a guide when distributing your ten points.

- *Me:* this is you indicating the areas to which your own attention is drawn – the things you naturally focus your time and energy on. If it helps, you could think of each of the ten points you're distributing representing five hours in a working week or five minutes in a one-hour meeting[26]. Again, be honest, and take your time. This isn't about the ideal you: it's about the real you. Notice which of the seven areas you're best known for attending to, the ones that energise you, the ones you procrastinate over, the ones you're most frustrated by when others focus too much or too little on them.

● *My current boss:* here you're showing where you think your current boss typically focuses their time and energy. Again, if it helps, use the 'one point equals 5 hours / 5 minutes' approach. Be fair, too. Don't just pick a recent week when your boss was particularly stressed or being forced to attend to one area more or less than usual. Think about the past few months, at least; longer if you can.

Example (ideal boss): if you wrote only "A good leader... knows their stuff and helps the people they lead develop their expertise" then the vast majority of your ten points would be placed on the third line in the table below ('Expertise'). If you wrote "A good leader gets results and should hold their people accountable for doing the same" *and* "... challenges the status quo, encouraging people to think creatively and question their own and others' fundamental assumptions", then you'd distribute most or all of your ten points across areas 4 and 5 (Achievement and Innovation). The more honest you are with yourself, indicating what you *are* looking for rather than what you think you *should* be looking for, the more helpful you'll find this whole process.

Potential areas of focus / task mind-set	My ideal boss	Me	My current boss
	distribute 10 points in total per column		
1 Opportunities: winning; finding loopholes; exerting influence / power over others			
2 Diplomacy: finding compromises; minimising conflict; promoting and displaying unity and loyalty; bringing people together socially			
3 Expertise: being a go-to person for logic, facts and knowledge; improving efficiency; getting the right answer; developing technical skills; broadening and/or deepening subject-matter expertise			
4 Achievement: driving for results; focusing on success; powering through adversity; achieving long-term goals; finding clever ways to overcome obstacles			
5 Innovation: breaking with convention; focusing on innovation and change; valuing difference and diversity of thought, thinking styles and perspectives; questioning own assumptions and ways of working and thinking			

Potential areas of focus / task mind-set	My ideal boss	Me	My current boss
	distribute 10 points in total per column		
6 Strategic transformation: seeing and simplifying the complexities of organisational life; challenging assumptions held across the organisation; stimulating change in others; blending vision with pragmatism; collaborating across departments for mutual gain, rather than protecting our own interests and/or pretending to collaborate and seeking to come out on top; triggering transformational change in others			
7 Societal transformation: transforming the way local, national and/or global communities think and operate; reinventing the organisation in historically significant ways			
8 Other...			

When you look at the table above…

What do you notice about the similarities and differences across the three columns? What are the implications?

....

....

....

....

Where does your image of the ideal boss come from? To what extent are your expectations logical and tailored to the needs of this organisation, this team and its operating environment? To what extent are they rooted in assumptions you're carrying from team to team that may or may not be correct in your current context?

....

....

....

In what ways does this notion of the ideal boss reflect your own focus? How does it enable and limit you? What are the implications for your relationships with this and future bosses?

....

....

....

....

In what ways do the similarities / differences between your task mind-set and your boss's enhance what the two of you contribute to the organisation – individually and together?

....

....

....

....

In what ways do the similarities / differences between your task mind-set and your boss's *inhibit* what the two of you contribute to the organisation – again, *individually and together*?

....

....

....

....

You might want to take a few moments to grab a drink, stretch your legs, get some air and think things through before we approach the third of these three ways of understanding your mind-set.

Your 'agency' mind-set

In addition to your task and relationship mind-set, your effectiveness with your boss and their effectiveness with you will be affected by your agency mind-set. What I mean by this is the combination of your expectations of the world and the extent to which you believe you

Optimistic vs
Pessimistic

Adaptable
vs Fixed

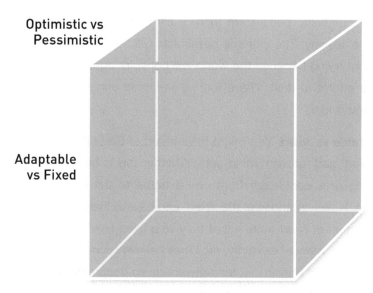

Proactive vs Reactive

(and your boss) can adapt to and influence the world around you. You might think of these as three axes, forming a cube. If you scored yourself on each axis relative to other people, you'd be placing yourself at a particular point in that cube.

There are similarities between the concepts that make up these three axes, but they *are* distinct, so let's take each in turn. Importantly, few of us will be at the same point within that cube in all situations and throughout our lives. We will have a natural position, though – a centre of gravity that's rarely shifted except by really significant life events. We'll also have our own triggers – events or people that can suddenly move us to somewhere else in the cube.

- ***Optimistic vs pessimistic.*** People with high levels of optimism are credited with living longer, recovering more quickly from injury and disease, with selling more[27] and with having more friends[28]. However, being too optimistic or too pessimistic can reduce our belief in our ability – or the need – to influence what happens to us.

Highly optimistic people are more likely to believe things will turn out fine anyway. The extreme pessimists will tell themselves there's no point trying because the world will conspire against us and turn all our efforts to dust. The evidence seems to suggest that neither extreme is ideal[29].

- **_Adaptable vs fixed._** You might have heard of Carol Dweck's work[30] on 'fixed' and 'growth' mind-sets. Whether this is binary, an either/ or thing or a continuum from one extreme to the other is up for debate. However, those at the 'fixed' end believe themselves to have a collection of fixed traits – that they've a fixed level of intelligence, confidence, manual dexterity, etc. They believe success comes from talent alone, so they invest far more energy in documenting or telling people about their talents than in developing those talents. In contrast, people at the 'adaptable' or 'growth' end of the scale believe that – through focus and hard work – they can build on the foundations of talent they've been given. They have a far greater hunger for learning than those with a fixed mind-set and Dweck argues that they're more resilient and achieve more.

- **_Proactive vs reactive._** Proactivity is generally rooted in a sense of self-efficacy[31] and a belief in our ability to influence outcomes. People with a more proactive mind-set believe success or failure (in a task, or in life) is largely or entirely down to them – whether that's their talents, their efforts or how well they combine the two. People with a more reactive mind-set place far greater weight on the influence of external factors and have less faith in their ability to affect what happens to them.

It's easy to confuse reactivity with pessimism, but they're different. One person could be optimistic and reactive, having complete faith that whatever they do everything will turn out for the best. Another person could be pessimistic and proactive, believing the world is a tough and dangerous place where everyone's out for themselves and the onus is on them to use all the skills and smarts at their disposal to come out in front in the rat race. Your boss is likely to want sufficient pessimism that you spot potential problems before they occur (but not so much that you're constantly scaring them or laden with doom and gloom) and sufficient proactivity that whenever you raise a problem you're also armed with potential solutions. That way you're shrinking the problem and making their life easier, rather than leaving them dreading the sight of you because every interaction leaves them with more problems and a longer to do list than they had before you arrived.

Where you fall on each of these three dimensions reflects and affects your expectations of yourself and the world around you and your boss. Is the world – and the world of work – a good place, a dangerous place or somewhere in the middle? Are you the master of your own fate, are you a rudderless boat adrift on the ocean of existence, or are there things in life that you can influence, things you can prepare for and surprising things you're just going to need to deal with? Are you generally capable, generally incapable, good at some things and worse at others, or as good as you choose to be? Do you play to win, play to avoid losing or play for the love of the game?

As you reflect on those questions, make a mark on each of the arrows below to show where you are currently on each of the three dimensions. As I said earlier, we all have our own centre of gravity where this agency mind-set is concerned – our own starting point in that cube. Similarly, each of us has our own set of triggers that can send us to somewhere else in the cube, sometimes in an instant.

When you've made the three marks for yourself, make a mark on each arrow to show where you think your boss is at the moment. If you're thinking about more than one boss, then either choose one or make marks for each of them.

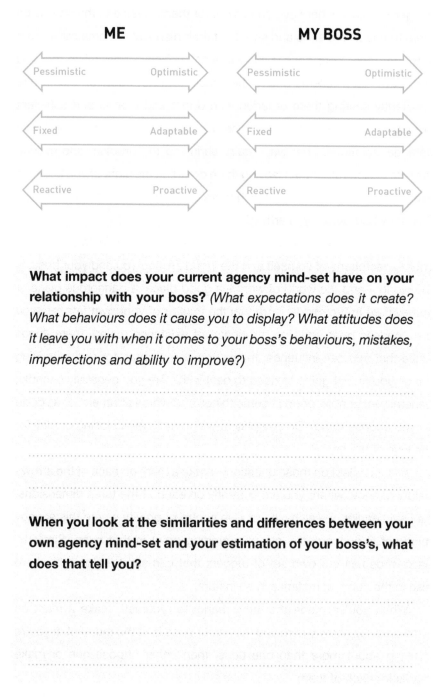

ME

Pessimistic — Optimistic

Fixed — Adaptable

Reactive — Proactive

MY BOSS

Pessimistic — Optimistic

Fixed — Adaptable

Reactive — Proactive

What impact does your current agency mind-set have on your relationship with your boss? *(What expectations does it create? What behaviours does it cause you to display? What attitudes does it leave you with when it comes to your boss's behaviours, mistakes, imperfections and ability to improve?)*

....

....

....

....

When you look at the similarities and differences between your own agency mind-set and your estimation of your boss's, what does that tell you?

....

....

....

From mind-set to action

In stepping back from yourself and examining your own mind-set through these three lenses – relationship, task and agency – you'll have seen ways in which your mind-set is enabling you to succeed and ways in which it could be inhibiting you from fulfilling your potential. I'm expecting you'll also have seen ways in which your mind-set is contributing positively to your relationships with the people who lead you and ways in which a tweak to that mind-set could make the relationship (even) more useful, rewarding and enjoyable for you and your boss – perhaps even for the people with whom you both work and the stakeholders you serve.

It's far harder to think ourselves into a new mind-set than it is to act our way into it. So I suggest you pause for a moment to write down 2-3 things you could do differently that would be evidence of bringing a more (or even more) productive mind-set to the relationship or relationships you're considering as you read this book.

Applying this lesson as a leader of others

If you're a leader in your own right, the way you completed that sentence "A good leader..." on page 57 will reflect and affect the way you lead your people. I'd expect you to be thinking already about the way your leadership of others is influenced by your assumptions and expectations about relationships, the kinds of tasks you and your people should be attending to, and your own sense of agency in the world.

I'd encourage you to ask yourself how the people you lead would have completed that sentence, focusing on each of them individually. What are their expectations of leaders in general? How have their past experiences of leadership – from childhood through to their last boss before you – affected the way they're approaching their relationship with you? What baggage are they bringing with them that has nothing to do with this current relationship but could be getting in the way? In what ways are you managing and struggling to live up to the model they have of their ideal boss? In what ways would it be realistic and beneficial for you to be more like that ideal boss, either in this relationship or more generally, without losing your authenticity? How might you help them help you to adapt or develop to be closer to that ideal? And, where their ideal is patently unachievable – for you at this point in time, or for any leader – how can you address that while maintaining their morale and commitment to you and your shared endeavours?

Looking at the three lenses we used to explore your mind-set regarding the people who lead you, it's worth considering the relationship mind-sets of the people you lead. You could do this for each individual in turn, or you could decide on the centre of gravity for the team as a whole. The same goes for your people's task mind-set (the things they believe you and they should be focusing on) and their agency mind-set. Whether you look at mind-set on an individual or collective basis, I'd encourage you to examine not just the norm, or the average mind-set, but the exceptions. What are the triggers that send them into a less productive mind-set? What impact does that have on performance, morale and commitment? When have they accessed a more productive mind-set? What impact has that had and what conditions enabled it to happen? Looking at the three ARC Qualities (see below), what impact does their prevailing mind-set have on their ability to be courageous, or take responsibility, or feel they can be authentic in their relationships with you and each other?

Of course, you'll also want to look at the impact of (or any similarities or differences between) your mind-set and theirs. What implications do those similarities and differences – and their expectations of you as their leader – have on their commitment? Or on the way they expect you to establish direction and the direction you and they will want to head in?

All of these are things you can focus on alone, reflecting on what you see, hear and feel when leading these people. They're also questions you can explore in conversation with the people you lead, either individually or collectively.

In summary

Despite research suggesting there's a base probability of 47% that a given manager will fail, there's a huge weight of expectation on the people 'in charge'. In this lesson, we looked at the ways in which you might be adding to both that weight and that probability of failure. We used three lenses to examine the mind-set with which you approach relationships with those who lead you:

- Relationships – the assumptions, expectations, beliefs and behaviours you bring to your interactions

- Tasks – the things you believe you and your boss should be doing

- Agency – your positive / negative expectations and your belief in your ability to adapt to and influence outcomes.

If you've worked through the various questions, you'll better understand the assumptions, beliefs and expectations you're bringing to these relationships. You'll have a sense of how that mind-set was formed, insight into the ways it's enabling and inhibiting you and ideas as to how to turn that insight into action.

●●●

Lesson 4:
We get the leader we deserve

- How you might be inadvertently derailing your boss

- Who's REALLY in control here?

- What do you and your boss really need from this relationship?

- What to do when your needs and your boss's needs clash

HAVE YOU EVER LISTENED to parents complaining about their children's behaviour and silently wondered why they can't see that it's their own behaviour that's causing the problem? Sometimes it's the same when people are complaining about the way their bosses treat them.

> **"...a [good] follower is a leader's steward every bit as much as a leader is the follower's steward"**
>
> Ira Chaleff in
> The Courageous Follower[32]

It's easy for outsiders to forget that leadership is difficult. As renowned thought leader Ira Chaleff[33] and others have observed, leading others is a challenge that can bring out the best and the worst in us. Leaders can find themselves losing their sense of authenticity and making more compromises than they'd like to – even when doing so means compromising their values. It's all too easy for the people they're leading (and for other observers) to watch with a sneer from the side-lines.

In any relationship there are patterns, or habits. New patterns form and old patterns fade away, but many patterns are pretty stable – so stable even that we take them with us from relationship to relationship. Some of those patterns or habits are helpful; some don't do much at all; others are impressively unhelpful. It's the latter we'll be focusing on here, with a specific focus on the ways in which your patterns and habits could be making it harder for your boss to lead you, work with you, get value from you, support, enable and develop you. At their most extreme, your habits may even be making it harder for them to simply survive in their role as your leader.

If you're inadvertently getting in your boss's way, then you're part of the problem and you may well continue to carry the same problems wherever you go, whoever your boss is. And if you're part of the problem, you're reducing your boss's (and potentially the rest of their people's) ability to add value to the organisation and its stakeholders. That's bad for them and it'll also probably reduce your own chances of succeeding – perhaps even of keeping your job. So we'll be focusing in this lesson on the unconscious drivers within you that could be causing you to undermine the quality and effectiveness of this relationship and the work you and your boss are trying to do.

Of course, you could be getting in your boss's way on purpose. If you've good reason to do so, you're likely living up to (or trying to live up to) Lessons 6 or 9, which call for us to take responsibility and show courage in the relationships we have with our bosses and other senior stakeholders.

If you're consciously and intentionally getting in the way and *don't* have a truly responsible reason for doing so, then I'd imagine there's a deeper problem and I'd encourage you to really challenge yourself, your motives and your assumptions. Lessons 1, 2 and 3 are a good place to start with that. This Lesson 4 is also a good way in, and 6 and 8 should help but they'll require you to have done some work on yourself with those first four lessons first.

Why would you be unconsciously derailing your boss?

You know that part of your brain that you think of as you? The part that has plans, that speaks to itself, that is filled with technical knowledge and prides itself on its forward thinking and the logical decisions it makes?

It's not actually you.

It doesn't really make all the decisions – at least not all of the ones that actually translate into action.

It's not really in control – not always, possibly not even most of the time.

'You' is a collection of integrated systems, with many of your behaviours and emotional reactions to the world guided by pretty primitive brain structures. The bit you call 'you' is the pre-frontal cortex (PFC), often called 'the CEO of the brain'. It's just inside your forehead, facing forward with little concept of what's happening behind and beneath it.

And then there's 'Amy'. Amy's what I call the collection of circuits that are focused on the immediate gratification of basic needs and the avoidance of pain. The name is short for 'amygdalae', the pair of structures that are central to fulfilling these fundamental needs. You might have come across the term 'amygdala hijack'[34] or heard Amy called 'the chimp'[35]. My clients tend to prefer Amy as a term as it's easier to work practically with the idea of a seven-year-old girl than with a chimp or a complex web of neurones. It also helps us appreciate that a lot of Amy's needs and ways of fulfilling them were 'programmed in' by our early life experiences, so it really is like a seven-year-old child is driving a lot of our emotions and behaviours.

Amy's location in the brain is important on a very practical level: she sits far closer to the parts of your brain that control your digestion, heart rate and breathing than your PFC does. She's right next to your memory stores, affecting both the retrieval of memories and the way your memories are encoded, and she has more neural connections to work with than the PFC. She has more, faster processing power and she thinks far more simply about things which makes decision-making far, far easier. Hence her ability to

'hijack' your behaviours despite your conscious mind's attempts to keep her in check.

So, Amy is a force to be reckoned with. She's there to protect you, to get you immediate gratification and protect you from harm. If she senses that your boss is an obstacle or a threat to either of those agendas, then she'll use everything in her armoury to remove or circumvent that obstacle and every trick in her thick black book to avoid or neutralise that threat. She'll play with your emotions, filter what you see and hear, tweak your memories and introduce a whole load of biases into your thinking, problem solving and decision-making processes. Yes, she really *can* do all that, but she honestly thinks she's doing it with your best interests at heart.

Oh, and your boss has an Amy, too.

Understanding Amy's dual agenda

If you answered the various questions I posed in Lesson 3, then you'll already have explored how your mind-set might be affecting your relationship with your boss. If you've worked through Lesson 2 ('Choose your leader wisely'), then you may have recognised in yourself some of the potential 'derailers' I suggested watching out for in a boss, in which case you should be thinking about how your own potential derailer behaviours could also be derailing your boss. Here we're shifting the focus onto the way your needs – or, really, Amy's needs – affect that relationship and your behaviours in it.

Needs are a huge thing in leadership. Having someone to lead us serves very powerful psychological needs for us[36]. For instance, it provides a sense of safety, order and certainty. It offers decisiveness, harmony and cohesion in the team and organisation, protecting us from ourselves and the chaos and barbarity we see in unfettered groups. Being led also means someone else does the hard work of bringing everyone's individual contributions together, of bearing 'the whole' in mind so we can attend to our own smaller pieces of reality. And when a leader fails to meet the needs of their people, they're usually eventually toppled. They're at least considered to have failed. Again, so much pressure on the leader to tick all the boxes...

There are lots of different ways to describe the things we need in life. The framework my clients find easiest to grasp and apply (called 'FIRO') suggests three fundamental human needs – inclusion, control and affection[37] – which together capture the simplicity and immediacy of Amy's dual agendas of immediate gratification and the avoidance of pain. Each of us has a different level of need in each of those areas. If any of those needs is underfed or overfed, we get uncomfortable, even stressed.

In addition, the creator of this FIRO framework, Will Schutz, points out that each of these three needs works in two directions: there's how much of it we need from others and how much we're keen to give out. So, I might be different to you in the extent to which I want to be included *and* the extent to which I want to include others. The same goes for the extent to which I want to control and be controlled, and the extent to which I want to express affection towards others and the extent to which I want them to show that they like or love me. Importantly, in a work context, affection is associated with a desire to share things about oneself – facts about our personal lives, how we feel, what we're really thinking about a particular relationship, and so on – and to have others share things about them.

Where do these needs come from? To some extent they'll be hard-wired into your basic biology. Largely they'll have been influenced by the culture you were born into, the way you were brought up and educated, and the way you've been treated as an adult – by bosses, colleagues, staff, friends and family.

What about all the other things I need and my boss needs from me, like 'getting results'?

We're looking at fundamental needs here. Frankly, Amy doesn't care about 'results' in the way an organisation would describe them any more than a small child does. Your Amy (and your boss's Amy) really only cares about the needs those 'results' meet for you. If your boss is hassling you to deliver, it's because if you fail to do so it'll undermine their ability to meet their needs for inclusion, control or openness in this relationship or another one. For example, they're worried they'll have to reprimand you, which could cause you not to like them; or they're afraid their inability to get results from you will cause them to seem incompetent in the eyes of others or show that they're not really in control.

Your needs on each of these three areas – inclusion, control and affection – will affect what you want from a given boss and how you act towards them. This will be exaggerated if we're not getting those needs met sufficiently elsewhere – in our relationships at work and in our personal lives. Amy was primed in infancy to rely on your parents to put things back in balance. Like it or not, now that we're adults, our Amys typically treat our bosses as our surrogate parents. Hence people's frequent overreliance on their bosses to ensure these fundamental needs get met. Your PFC might notice what she's up to; it might not. So you may be consciously aware that your behaviours are driven by a need to feel significant, competent or liked; or you might be operating in blissful ignorance, assuming you're doing what any sensible person would do in your situation.

At the same time, our behaviours and those of our colleagues will be meeting or failing to meet our bosses' needs for inclusion, control and affection. The following three case studies will show you how this can play out.

Case study: when our needs for inclusion are out of sync

Mike has a high need for inclusion, so he likes to be invited to lots of meetings and worries when people are exchanging information without including him. His boss, Pav, has much lower inclusion needs. Mike's cc'ing her on everything and involving her in every decision, while at the same time fretting that Pav doesn't keep him sufficiently up to date and involve him in important decisions. Pav feels overwhelmed at first, then frustrated. She begins to doubt Mike's ability to filter, prioritise, delegate and work autonomously. So she focuses her attention on the members of her team that make her life easier. Mike feels excluded and becomes increasingly frustrated and demoralised. He complains to others that Pav is playing favourites and failing to keep sufficiently on top of the detail.

Keen to take a proactive approach to the situation, Mike starts to go around her to more senior figures, including Pav's own boss Neal, who has more similar inclusion needs to Mike's. Neal is initially keen that Mike respect the chain of command, but he can't help but agree that Pav isn't as inclusive as Neal would like her to be. Mike meets a need for Neal that Pav hasn't been meeting. So Neal feels increasingly drawn to Mike as someone who'll keep him in the loop. It's not long before, between them, they're doing to Pav what they'd hate anyone to do to them: they're excluding her. For a while, Pav barely notices: she's vaguely aware that neither Mike nor Neal is hassling her the way they used to, and at first it's a relief. Then she's cut out of one conversation too many. She investigates, concludes that Mike has been criticising and undermining her, trying to take her job. So she goes on the offensive to protect her future. Three months later, Mike finds himself out of a job.

Case study: when our control needs clash

Jenny has low control needs. She prefers to operate independently, with minimal direction from above and with no responsibility for exerting control over anyone else. Her boss, Alberto, shares her preference for a life free from control by higher authorities. However, that's because he likes things done his way: he has a need to be in control, but not be controlled. Jenny sees their similarities but finds it hard to understand why Alberto won't give her the same freedom Alberto demands from his own boss. She assumes it's because Alberto doesn't think she's competent, so Jenny works harder and harder to add value, hoping to break the chains.

Alberto worries that Jenny is overstretching herself, so he introduces more safeguards, effectively tightening those chains. So Jenny starts to find ways to assert her independence, bending the rules and 'seeking forgiveness, rather than permission'. And so the spiral continues. Eventually, because our control needs are closely linked to our attitudes to competence, Jenny is forced to make a choice – probably unconscious – between seeing herself as lacking the competence to earn Alberto's trust or seeing his smothering leadership style as evidence that Alberto is the one lacking sufficient competence to do his job.

Case study: when our needs for affection are misaligned

Oscar has a higher-than-average need for affection. His friends, family and workmates see him as warm, affable, a little 'soft' sometimes, and open – sometimes too open – about his life outside work. His colleague Farah, who shares the same boss, has lower-than-average needs in this area. She doesn't want to be *disliked* at work, but she's more private than Oscar, with a handful of close confidants, only one of whom works in their organisation. She's seen as somewhat formal and usually focuses conversation on the task at hand. Their boss Brad's affection needs come somewhere in between. While he respects Farah's right to keep her private life to herself, he finds it harder to like and trust her because he doesn't feel he really knows her. When Brad asks about her weekend or how she is, Farah is brief and fairly vague. He has a greater sense of common ground with Oscar because he's met Oscar's wife and they've children the same age. He has no idea that he actually has more in common with Farah: among other things, they're both keen cyclists and are divorced with difficult relationships with their exes.

Oscar's need to be close to people drives him to ask Brad lots of questions. Some feel pretty invasive but Brad has few people he feels he can talk to, so he finds himself opening up about the challenges with his ex-wife. The conversation evolves into lunches and drinks after work. Farah sees them bonding and, while she doesn't want to be close friends with either of them, she becomes increasingly sensitive to any signs of favouritism. Despite the lack of any overt racism or sexism from either of them, it's hard for her and her confidants to ignore the fact that she's a woman of Saudi descent and Brad and Oscar are two white males. Then, one day, Oscar's natural openness causes him to tell her something that Brad told him in confidence regarding his aspirations for the team. It's a small thing and in other circumstances it would have caused nothing more than a ripple. However, with Farah sensitised and Brad already finding it hard to understand and trust her motives, that small indiscretion triggers a series of events that involve HR, poison all three relationships and end in one of the three leaving the company.

In all three of those cases, a better understanding of each other's needs would have made a massive difference to the outcomes and the relationship between the individuals involved and their bosses. So I'd encourage you to take some time now to use the following questions to help you reflect on the role your needs and those of your current boss(es) play in the way you work together.

What are your needs in these three areas (inclusion, control and affection) and how well are they being met at the moment, at work and generally in life? *(There are tools you can use to measure this directly. The details, should you want them, are in the notes at the end of this book[38].)*

What might you be unconsciously assuming about your boss's responsibility for meeting your needs for inclusion, control and affection?

....

....

....

....

....

....

....

Based on their behaviours in this relationship and others, what do you think your boss's needs are in each of these three areas? What similarities, differences and (potentially) conflicting needs do you see?

....

....

....

....

....

....

....

How might your (conscious or unconscious) attempts to get your needs met be affecting your boss's behaviours towards you?

....

....

....

....

....

....

To help you understand your own patterns and take control of them, rather than letting them (and Amy) control you: to what extent does the pattern you have created between you and your boss echo a pattern created earlier in your life – for example, in your relationship with a parent, grandparent or other significant adult?

....

....

....

....

....

....

....

What to do if your needs are misaligned

If your needs and your boss's clash and it's proving problematic, then essentially you've four options. For each, I've highlighted which other lessons could help you take it forward – bearing in mind, of course, that the nature of the clash and profile of unmet needs will affect the extent to which that particular lesson will help you with this particular situation.

1 **Adapt your approach** perhaps by finding a way to get your unmet needs fulfilled in other relationships or by finding a way to operate effectively and stay sufficiently happy and committed without those needs being met

2 **Find a way to encourage them to adapt their approach,** either by getting their own unmet needs met by someone else or genuinely accepting that your needs will have to take precedence over theirs

Approaches 1 and 2 will both benefit from:

- Lesson 5 ('Seek clarity') if it's an issue of control, clarity of purpose, delegation or who to include

- Lesson 6 ('Take due responsibility') if the clash touches on matters of trust or who should and shouldn't take responsibility

- Lesson 7 ('Continually build your capacity') if the challenge is related to perceptions or feelings of (in)competence on your part or theirs

- Lesson 8 ('Secure and maintain commitment') if unmet needs are an obstacle to engagement or buy-in

- Lesson 9 ('Be courageous') if the difficulty lies in finding ways to challenge other people or the status quo

3	*Find a way to get their needs met without reducing your ability to meet yours,* by which I don't mean 'compromise', which is just a combination of options 1 and 2	• Lesson 3 ('Challenge your assumptions') offers a starting point for a conversation with your boss about what each of you expects from the relationship
		• Lesson 5 ('Seek clarity') can help you ascertain the optimal ways of working together when planning a piece of work
		• Lesson 6 ('Take due responsibility'), particularly the section on trust as the more trust you have in the relationship the easier it will be to address this current challenge
		• Lesson 9 ('Be courageous'), because finding a creative, collaborative way of meeting both parties' needs can take courage on both sides
		• Lesson 10 ('Promote and enable good followership in others'), because it'll bring you allies when it comes to meeting your boss's needs (and your own) which reduces the pressure on you
4	*Find a new leader,* escaping the situation in favour of one in which you're more likely to get your needs met	• Lesson 2 ('Choose your leader wisely'), but I'd work through the rest of the lessons before seeking a new boss as otherwise you might find you've taken your problems with you

If you're keen on option 3 and want to find ways to get your boss's needs met without reducing your ability to meet yours, I'd recommend drawing a map of your boss's world to help you clarify your understand of the pressures placed on him or her, the impact this has on their ability to get their needs met, and the people around them who are either helping or hindering in that regard. Take a big blank piece of paper, or use the space on the next page. Write your boss's name at the centre, with a small bubble around it. Then add the people who report into them, including yourself, with each individual in their own small bubble, then your boss's more senior stakeholders and peers, then any other projects they have on their plate. Finally, add whatever factors you're aware of in their life outside work that'll make it easier or harder to get their needs met.

Once you have that map, draw a line between your boss and each other person on the map. Then look at each line and mark next to it the ways in which that relationship places demands on your boss and the ways in which it helps them get their own needs met. You might also want to use an arrow on that line to show the balance of give and take in the relationship: if the arrow is pointing towards your boss, they're taking more than is being taken from them; if the arrow points away, they're giving more than they're gaining from the relationship. When you're done, look for lines on that map that you could influence in some way to help your boss get their needs met without you having to sacrifice yours.

Your map

Whether or not you've created that map, if you've identified ways in which your needs (or clashes between your needs and your boss's needs) are limiting the effectiveness of this relationship, take some time to reflect on the thinking you've done since we started this lesson. Then note down the things you could do or discuss with your boss to improve things.

Applying this lesson as a leader of others

If you're a leader in your own right, you'll probably have been thinking about the mismatches and potential mismatches between your needs and those of the people you lead. If we think of your leadership in terms of The Three Core Disciplines and ARC Qualities, we can see for instance that the extent to which you need to feel in control will affect the ways in which you Establish Direction. The stronger your need to feel in control, the more likely you are to dictate that direction and the less likely you are to want to give

that power to others. Similarly, the higher your need for inclusion, the more likely you are to involve others in the conversation – although, of course, your control needs will influence the extent to which that conversation is a collaboration or more of an opportunity for them to ask questions and raise concerns about the direction you've already decided.

Similarly, because our need for affection influences how much we're willing to share of ourselves, you'll find your needs in that area will have an effect on people's experiences of your authenticity. This isn't entirely fair, as you could be entirely authentic in your desire to keep things private. However, we're talking about how people experience you and people with higher affection needs may find it harder to believe they're seeing the whole, real you if you're more private than they'd like. The flipside, of course, is that a leader who's overly open and overly preoccupied with being liked can seem inauthentic, too. Not only that, but they can appear insufficiently responsible and/or courageous because they're likely to find it harder to challenge underperformance and hold people to account.

All of these things can make it harder to secure people's commitment, which – as we'll see in Lesson 8 – relies, among other things, on trust, productive conflict and a sense of accountability. Our needs have a direct impact on commitment, too, though. If you're trying to take your people in a direction that's inconsistent with their needs then they'll struggle to commit. You'll see this, for instance, where leaders are trying to take their people in a new direction or get them to take on additional responsibilities where that direction or those responsibilities require them to:

- Replace old allegiances with new (inclusion)
- Embrace new skills or ways of working (control), or
- Do something that might make them unpopular (affection).

So, I'd encourage you to think about how your needs – which includes meeting your stakeholders' needs – are aligned and misaligned with those of the people you lead. Where they clash, there's increased potential for you to be at odds with each other – openly or covertly, consciously or unconsciously. So, whenever you sense a clash, I'd recommend taking action.

In summary

In this lesson, we've looked at ways in which your needs might clash with those of your boss, which will increase your chances of getting in each other's way.

We looked at how 'Amy' – your unconscious – can have a positive or negative impact on your relationship with your boss. We identified three fundamental human needs: to be included, to feel in control and to feel liked or loved. If you answered the questions I posed, you'll have seen how your needs influence your behaviours and how the similarities and differences between your needs and your boss's can help or hinder you.

•●•

5

Lesson 5: Seek clarity

• • •

- How can anyone score a goal if they can't see the goalposts?

- Why clarity is as much your responsibility as your boss's

- How to use the Five-Phase Framework and Seven Levels of Delegation to seek, gain and maintain clarity

- What to do if you're still struggling for clarity

AS WE'VE SEEN ELSEWHERE in this book, one of the Three Core

Disciplines that enable leaders and the people they lead to excel is Establishing Direction. Critically, that direction not only needs to be the *right* direction – i.e. the right or best choice given the context – it needs to be clear and properly understood. Otherwise, it's impossible for people to fully commit, line up the necessary resources or decide on the right actions to take in pursuit of that goal. It sounds *so* simple, but I've worked with a lot of teams over the years who have lacked

> "If you don't know where you're going, you will probably end up somewhere else"
>
> Laurence J. Peter, author of *The Peter Principle: why things always go wrong*[39]

true, shared clarity on their vision, mission, roles and/or collective and individual objectives. For example:

- One team leading a group of companies dithered for years over whether to merge two of those organisations into one. When the chairman and CEO asked me to come and work with them, it was apparent that the lack of a clear, final decision was undermining the performance of both businesses. The two organisations were already collaborating in some areas, but they were delaying creating robust processes to maximise the efficiency of that collaboration because nobody knew whether or when those processes might need to change. At the same time, one of the company heads was determined to prove that his business should stand on its own, rather than being merged with the other. Unsurprisingly, this mind-set filtered down to his staff and encouraged habits and silo-thinking that undermined and/or reduced the value of collaboration with the other company.

- The executive board of a public sector organisation showed a distinct lack of accountability, for behaviours as well as results. We gave each member of the team a coach and a separate coach worked with the team as a whole. In my early coaching sessions with the CEO, his frustration with his colleagues' failure to deliver was palpable. He was clear on his expectations of them and equally clear – with me at least – on the ways in which they were failing to meet those expectations. However, it became clear through my discussions with the other coaches that the clarity he had in his own mind wasn't translating into clarity for the team. They weren't sufficiently clear what he expected them to deliver and how he expected them to behave, which made it difficult for them to deliver on his expectations. Not only that, but it gave them a great deal more scope for dodging accountability

> when they *did* know they'd failed to deliver. After all, if there was no explicit agreement on the boundaries of acceptable behaviour and performance, how could they possibly be outside those boundaries?

At an individual level, lack of clarity reduces people's commitment to their work, boss and organisations. It can undermine their self-esteem and it's a contributing factor to dissatisfaction – not just with work, but with life in general. At its worst, lack of clarity can increase our chances of suffering from depression[40]. We have a fundamental need to feel a sense of control and understand what is expected of us. Without it, we fall into a state of 'learned helplessness', in which we lose all belief in our ability to affect what happens to us. So, this section of the book is not just about your work, development and career progression; it's about your health.

When it comes to performance as a team or organisation, clarity becomes increasingly important – and increasingly difficult – as the operating environment becomes increasingly changeable / volatile, uncertain, complex and ambiguous. The more 'VUCA' the context, the more important it becomes for people at more junior grades in an organisation to be responsive and adaptable. Without clarity, though, that responsiveness and adaptability can descend into chaos; create unnecessary or even crippling risk and inefficiency; overwhelm people with too much responsibility or by taking them beyond their capabilities; undermine important policies, protocols, values and even an organisation's core brand; destroy economies of scale... the list goes on.

A Five-Phase Framework for achieving and maintaining clarity

A few years ago, I developed a Five-Phase Framework for my colleagues and me to use with the teams we were coaching. I've since found it enormously helpful in a range of contexts. It draws on a wealth of research models and insights into best practice from a whole host of different disciplines including project management, organisational change, executive coaching, the Agile movement and the military's 'intelligence cycle'[41] and Mission Command model[42].

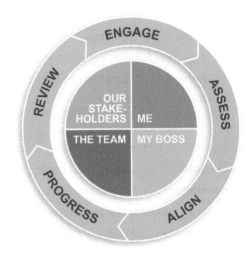

The central idea of the Five-Phase Framework (see above) is this: regardless of its scale, there are five critical phases to any piece of work: Engage, Assess, Align, Progress, Review.

At each of those phases there are a number of people we need to be thinking about and potentially involving. In this case, those people are you, your boss, the stakeholders who have a vested interest in the piece of work and the wider team.

You can use the framework with your boss, the people you lead or other stakeholders – it's as much a leadership tool as it is a tool for working effectively with people in more senior positions. If the work is fairly straightforward, I'd recommend working through all five phases in one sitting – perhaps using the image above as a way of holding the framework in mind. If it's especially complex, you'll likely benefit from working through a few iterations together, taking time out in between to reflect, recalibrate and gather additional information.

Phase One: Engage

This is the part where we get people on board with what we're meant to be doing. It's sometimes easy to leave this part to our leaders, rather than taking responsibility for it ourselves. If I'm adding real value, though, I'll proactively engage myself and my boss by bringing us together to talk about the piece of work in question and show them I'm going to be making life easier for them.

Where clarity is concerned, I need to get clarity on my boss's overall intent and how this intent aligns with the intentions of their own superiors. For *real* clarity, I'll want to extend that process to my stakeholders in general. I'll also want to know that this piece of work is high up those people's lists of priorities. Otherwise, I'm likely to struggle to get the support I need to ensure it succeeds.

The more I know about what my boss's boss was intending when she briefed my boss, the easier it'll be for me to be purposefully creative and adaptable without undermining our collective endeavour. This is particularly important in environments that are complex, unpredictable and/or ambiguous. To use a military example, if I've been asked to defend a particular hill because my boss's boss wants to stop the enemy taking the town on the other side of it, I'll know that I may need to move to another hill if the enemy unexpectedly comes from the opposite direction. If I'm not clear on the *reason* for defending the hill, I'll just sit there on top of it as the town burns below, expecting to be rewarded for the fact that the enemy never engaged me in battle.

I'll also increase my chances of success without overextending myself if I get clarity on what my boss considers to be the minimum criteria for success in this endeavour – similar to what the British Army calls the Main Effort and proponents of the Agile methodology call the Minimum Viable Product[43]. That might sound under-ambitious, like "What's the very least I need to achieve here in order to scrape through with minimal effort?" However, it's this clarity that will help me understand where to draw the line on quality, timelines and resources. It's also a useful counter to perfectionism and scope creep, both of which are rife in the organisations I've encountered – and both of which increase stress and reduce efficiency, effectiveness and overall performance.

All too often, bosses fail to clearly prioritise when delegating work to others. Like many people in organisations, they act as if everything's equally urgent and equally important. It can't be. To help prevent the stress and mess this can cause, it's important to ask them to identify the activity they believe is crucial to the success of the overall endeavour at that point in time and should therefore be first in line when it comes to allocating energy and resources. This prioritisation might change as the situation evolves but it's essential that any changes are made clearly and consciously, with both parties involved. Having a single Main Effort makes a huge difference in any relationship, but even more effective is to establish a clear ranking of the top five priorities and revisit these periodically. You may meet resistance in trying to get this – we'll look at why shortly – but if you and your boss can't get past this, you'll be conspiring to create problems for yourselves further down the line.

Understanding my boss and stakeholder's intent, the Main Effort and the minimum criteria for success means I know what effect I'm supposed to achieve and why it needs to be achieved. I'm not asking *how* it needs to be achieved: if the delegation is working properly, that *how* should be up to me – and we'll come back to that in a moment. We'll also look at reasons you might struggle to get clarity at any of these five phases.

Finally, this initial Engage phase asks that we think about the rest of the team. What clarity do they need from the outset? This might include my boss or me making it clear to the rest of the team where my role and remit begins and ends in relation to this work, what our aspirations are for the work and what I might need from the team to make it happen. After all, in high performing teams, everyone understands everyone else's role, responsibilities and challenges.

To help you put the Engage phase into practice, I'd encourage you to think of a current piece of work and complete the table below in order to check and enhance the degree of clarity you have with regard to people's engagement and how you'll need to manage it going forward.

Some suggestions as you approach this:

- If you've more stakeholders than columns, or need more space, then do the work on a separate sheet or sheets, or download the Excel spreadsheet from the Boss Factor resources page at www.leaderspace.com

- You might also want to share and discuss this table with your boss – either after you've completed it or as you work through it

- Once you've ascertained the explicit and unspoken priorities, needs and expectations for a given stakeholder, it's well worth ranking them so you have a clear understanding of what's most important to them. You'll have a single ranking across both the explicit and unspoken boxes for a single stakeholder. Of course, you can do the ranking yourself or you can work through the ranking with that stakeholder or with someone else.

- To help you manage expectations going forward, it'll help if you agree how involved each stakeholder will need to be as the work progresses. Do they need to be informed at each decision point or only at key milestones? Is the expectation that they're kept updated, that they'll provide input or be involved in the decision-making? Do they have powers of veto? And what are your expectations of them when it comes to updating you on things they're hearing about the work or that might affect its chances of success?

If for some reason you'd rather not use the table, you might prefer to create your own checklist for the Engage phase. I'll be suggesting this for all five phases towards the end of this lesson, so you'll find space on page 122 for recording your ideas.

Stakeholder	Me
Explicit priorities, needs and expectations (what they're saying)	
Unspoken priorities, needs and expectations (the things they're not saying)	
What do they believe is the 'Main Effort' / minimum criteria for success?	
How much do they benefit if this work succeeds (0 – 5)*?	
How much do they lose if it fails (0 – 5)?**	
How engaged are they at the moment (0 – 5?)***	
How involved do they need to be?	
Actions required	

*   score from 0 - 5; use a minus number if it's in their interest that it fails
**   use minus numbers if it would be harmful to them if this work succeeds
*** use minus numbers if they're actively disengaged

My Boss ....

Phase Two: Assess

This is where we ascertain the gap between where we are now and where we need to be. For example:

- **Resources (people, equipment, budget, etc.).** What do I need? What do I currently have available to me? How might my available resources change over the course of this work? What scope do I have for accessing additional resources if necessary and how would I go about that?

- **Enablers and supporters.** Who is actively supporting what we're doing? What support are they providing or offering (advocacy, advice, practical assistance, influence, etc.) Who has supported this in the past and for what reason are they no longer doing so? Who could potentially start or stop supporting us in the future? Similarly, what other internal and external factors does my boss already know will, or could, help make this happen?

- **Risks and blockers.** Who's resisting already or could potentially derail what we're trying to achieve? What are the key risks that my boss is already aware of? What upcoming events could potentially impact our success? What past events could have left residual effects that might reduce our chances of success? What's happening elsewhere in the organisation (or outside of it) that could draw resources or support away from what we're doing?

The more complex the task, the more time and energy I'd invest in answering these questions. I'd be expecting to do a fair amount of the assessment myself, but my boss will have a lot of useful information already, so it's well worth exploring this at the outset. Similarly, I'd be remembering to ask these questions in relation to the team, whether that's the team I'm leading or my team of peers.

Thinking of a current piece of work – ideally the same one you considered in the Engage phase – take a few moments to describe the gap between where you are now and where you need to be, using the questions above to stimulate your thinking.

....

....

....

....

....

....

Phase Three: Align

Once we've assessed the gap between our aspirations and our current reality, we need to decide how we're going to close that gap. However we plan to do it, we're going to have a hard time putting that plan into action if it's not aligned with the needs, agendas and actions of our stakeholders – and particularly our boss. Very few bosses will genuinely give us the license to do whatever we want – those that do are generally pretty ineffective leaders. So, while there's a lot to be said for leaders giving their people autonomy, it's always wise to ensure a clear and up-to-date shared understanding of the extent of that autonomy and what means are justified in achieving our objectives.

For instance, I remember asking the owners of a 250-person business what they expected of its Managing Director – he was in the room at the time. Their initial response was a nice clear profitability target. That was it, they assured us both.

"So," I said, "if he hits that target by ditching IT services [their core offering] and switching to selling golf clubs, that'd be okay?"

No, they said; it wouldn't. In fact, not only did he need to stay true to the original vision for the company, but they wanted to subject him to quarterly reviews, which would include an assessment of his impact as a leader within the organisation. Lucky we cleared that up early, then, as they'd have ousted him if he'd brought in the money but failed to deliver on those previously unspoken expectations.

Unlike that Managing Director – at least until we had that conversation – many commercial aircraft pilots benefit from very immediate, explicit and visible clarity regarding what are considered optimal and acceptable parameters: a 'tunnel in the sky' shown on the cockpit's head-up display. This shows the ideal route to their destination given the current conditions, but it's a fairly broad tunnel and the pilot is left in control. It's helpful for leaders and the people they lead to have some equivalent, some guardrails that provide clarity on any 'must have' courses of action and any courses of action that would be absolute no-nos. These benefit both parties: they limit the potential fallout for your boss and reduce the amount of damage you can do yourself and the project, while increasing the extent to which your boss can hand you control and autonomy which empowers you and makes life easier for them.

Two final points when it comes to aligning. Firstly, it can be helpful to ascertain early on what help your boss is willing or expecting to give you when it comes to ensuring the team and your other stakeholders are sufficiently aligned with the decisions you make.

Secondly, I'd recommend exploring with your boss the possibility that there may be things they cannot share with you for some reason. Showing that you understand this reduces the tension they're likely to be feeling if there *is* information they need to withhold. It also allows you to work together to find creative ways to ensure that your decisions and actions are still aligned to the various agendas in play and would still make sense were you apprised of that missing information. For instance, you might agree on a 'proxy' for that information – a substitute that you both know is false but is close enough to the truth to enable you to operate as efficiently and effectively as you would if you knew it. By way of example, I once coached someone who had a non-work issue that they didn't wish to share, but which we had to factor in if our work was to succeed. I asked her to give it a name and she called it 'Kevin'. From then on, we were able to check the impact of Kevin on things we were discussing without me ever having to know what Kevin actually was.

Returning to the piece of work you've been thinking about as you've worked through this lesson, what are the key things you need to consider and do to ensure you've sufficient, genuine clarity at the Align phase?

Phase Four: Progress

This is the phase where most of what is considered the 'actual work' gets done. The British Army's advice here is that the leader should have minimal control measures in place, to avoid placing unnecessary limits on their 'subordinates'. This is in spite of precision being pretty important in military contexts - in terms of objectives, outcomes and the way those outcomes are delivered with minimal loss of life. So I believe the same 'minimal control methods' approach applies in civilian contexts, too. Importantly, though, 'minimal' means 'optimal' not 'recklessly absent'.

The following Seven Levels of Delegation[44] can really help here. They're a way of clarifying the degree of decision-making authority our bosses are giving us, rather than making assumptions and risking those assumptions being misaligned. It's particularly useful during this phase as it should be an iterative agreement, evolving as the work evolves and the environment around you changes. It also helps your boss to gradually let go of responsibility, particularly if they're finding that difficult – more on that in Lesson 6. The Seven Levels are as follows:

1. **They tell you what to do:** they assess the problem, decide the best course of action and issue the instructions. They might explain their rationale. They might invite questions so they and you can be sure you understand what they're expecting from you, but the instruction itself is not debatable.

2. **They ask you for the data they need to make a decision:** they ask for your analysis of the problem but not your proposals for solving the problem. They then review your analysis, decide what needs to be done and explain their rationale to you.

3. **You offer options:** they ask for your analysis of the problem (or perhaps present their own analysis of it) and your ideas for potential solutions, plus the pros and cons of each. Then they choose from between those options (or integrate your ideas into an

alternative), explain their decision and ask you to proceed with that course of action.

4. ***You offer a single recommendation:*** they ask you to analyse the problem, work out the optimal solution and come to them for approval to put that solution into action. They then explain their reasons for giving or withholding that approval.

5. ***You check your decisions before moving forward:*** they leave it to you but ask that you keep them informed of your decisions, actions and rationale before you proceed so they can raise their concerns beforehand if they have any. Ideally you should give them a realistic deadline for raising those concerns, after which you can assume it's okay to proceed.

6. ***You get on with it and report back:*** they leave it to you and ask only that you keep them updated on what you've done and why you chose to do it. As with Level 5, they are still accountable for anything that goes wrong, but can take very little credit for what goes well.

7. ***Full autonomy:*** they step back and you get on with it with their full, public endorsement. You don't check with them, you don't involve them in identifying problems or resolving them. If you do report back to them, it's with a single bullet point stating what was achieved, so they know you've actually been doing something. They are still fully accountable for oversight of your work.

Getting clarity from your boss on which level you're meant to be at can be enormously helpful, bearing in mind that you could potentially agree different levels for different kinds of decision. However, few bosses are sufficiently clear or proactive in this regard. It's one of the reasons they find it so hard to delegate. When they operate at too low a level, they're micromanaging and stifling their people. When they operate at too high a level, things go wrong and they let their own bosses down, so they typically swing back the other way and overshoot the ideal balance of autonomy and oversight. The decision as to which is the right level will depend on an assessment of:

- The riskiness of the work, in terms of the likelihood of it going wrong and the impact if it does

- The extent to which you have the capacity to deliver it (see Lesson 7, Continually Build Your Capacity)

- Your commitment to the work (see Lesson 8, Secure and Maintain Commitment)

- The volatility, uncertainty, complexity and ambiguity of the environment in which you're working.

Which levels best describe the way your current boss delegates to you?

What factors encourage them to operate at that level (or those levels)?

What would you change, and how would you do that?

It's also worth remembering, when working with these Seven Levels of Delegation, that there might be any number of reasons why your boss has suddenly moved from one level to another. Some reasons might be directly related to you – whether it's about the commitment you're showing or the capacity you're displaying, or something else. Other reasons will have nothing at all to do with you. We'll explore this further in Lesson 6 when we look more closely at how responsibility does and doesn't get shared between leaders and the people they lead.

When looking at this Progress phase in advance, it can be helpful to brainstorm the kinds of situations that might justifiably raise the need for your boss to intervene or for you to seek help. You might, for instance, introduce some form of risk assessment that identifies ways in which each of those risks could be removed, reduced, managed or mitigated. Depending on the circumstances, it can also help to create some mutual understanding of the kind of help that could be made available if it's needed.

You'll also want to agree, and continue to revisit, your own and your stakeholders' attitude to failures and delays. The Agile methodology calls for 'failing fast'. This is really a shorthand for creating quick, efficient experiments and ensuring each tells us something useful, whether it succeeds or fails. So I'd encourage you to seek (and periodically recalibrate) clarity on how best to experiment and quickly learn from those experiments whether they fail or (hopefully) succeed – as well as clarity on the extent to which such experiments are acceptable.

Being Agile also means trialling multiple approaches simultaneously so we don't place all our eggs in one basket. For example, a software developer once told me that, all too often, his client organisations were determined to invest all of their budget in building one technology platform through which to communicate with their customers, ignoring the fact that they already knew that different customers prefer to use different platforms for different things: desktop or mobile browsers for some interactions, phone or webchat for others – and then there's SMS, email, instant messaging, Facebook, Twitter, dedicated apps and so on. This single, linear approach was a key reason, the developer said, for so many organisations failing to properly engage with their customers. So I'd encourage clarifying the extent to which parallel activities are permissible (or tolerable) and re-clarifying as you go.

Finally, remember that – at each phase – we need to attend to all four of the boxes at the centre of the Five-Phase Framework. In the Progress phase, it's critical to ensure that there are no unpleasant surprises for our team or stakeholders.

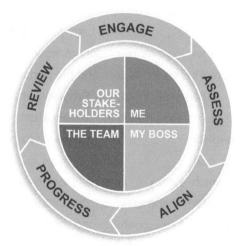

Phase Five: Review

The Five-Phase Framework makes it look like the Review phase comes at the end. In reality, the framework is iterative and most of us go through numerous five-phase processes in parallel over different time spans. One might last a year, another a month; another might run its course in a single meeting.

At the same time, it's certainly worth agreeing review processes upfront. There's obvious stuff like key milestones and key performance indicators, but it's always worth exploring and agreeing when and how we're going to report back on the progress we're making. After all, people differ considerably in their needs for information, both in terms of the frequency they require and the level of detail they're looking for. And people's needs often differ from project to project, relationship to relationship – particularly as the external pressure they're under waxes and wanes.

Importantly, it's the nature of any endeavour that things change. New information comes to light; people join or leave; resources appear, change and disappear; people's circumstances evolve, altering what they need from you, the project and each other; objectives can change entirely, sometimes without essential people noticing. Building in the right review processes helps us stay on top of these changes and adapt to them.

The Review phase sits at the core of the Agile methodology. As you may or may not know, Agile teams have regular 'retrospectives' which will typically bring the team – and potentially its core stakeholders – together around a handful of key questions, to which everyone is expected to contribute answers. This is *really* good practice. I'd suggest working up your own key questions as they'll be tailored to your context and relationships, but you might draw on the following for inspiration:[45]

- What's gone well since our last review?

- What's gone less well than we'd have hoped?

- What should we do differently next time?

- What one small change would make a big difference?

- What assumptions have we been making and how can we test those?

- Who are we not sufficiently involving / engaging / communicating with? (Or, who are we involving too much?)

- What is puzzling us / the team / our stakeholders? (Or, what are we / they struggling to understand?)

- Who do we want / need to thank?

You'll notice they're all open questions and none of them ask 'Why?' Asking 'Why?' tends to provoke defensiveness, so questions that start with that particular word are best avoided, or at least used carefully.

What questions would you ask? Of whom would you ask them? And when?

....

....

....

....

....

....

Trouble getting clarity?

Sometimes we're doing our best to get clarity but it's just not forthcoming.

I once coached the German CFO of a division of a well-known multinational – let's call him Christoff. Christoff was on a contract with a long notice period, rather than being fully employed by the organisation. He wanted clarity from his boss in the parent organisation regarding the likely length of that contract, so that – if necessary – he could start looking for another job. His boss appeared to be dodging the question and Christoff was growing increasingly frustrated.

We brainstormed and explored a number of reasons why a boss might not be as clear as we'd like them to be. Those reasons might vary from phase to phase, but they're going to come from one of four sources:

- **Your boss.** Some years ago, I thought I was giving my team latitude, when I was actually failing to be sufficiently clear because I didn't have clarity in my own mind. I felt behind on a project from the start and unable to clear enough time to do the planning I knew was needed. So I was hedging my bets, delaying giving clarity until I could be more certain what I wanted from them. From my team's perspective,

I wasn't giving them freedom, I was avoiding telling them where the goal posts were so I could then move them once we'd kicked the ball far enough across the field. Some bosses will fail to give sufficient clarity for similar reasons. Others might be withholding information because they're afraid to share it, bored of sharing it or think they have already been clear enough. Others might lack sufficient confidence to be clear, fearing they'll be seen as bossy or controlling. Others may lack or feel they lack the communication skills to be sufficiently clear.

- **You.** Maybe your need for clarity is different from theirs and they've already given what they think is reasonable. Perhaps you want more detail than they're used to giving, or you like to think further ahead than they do, or you need more of the bigger picture than they'd think to offer. Christoff was a highly confident, assertive, focused and career-driven man with a very strong need to feel in control and a tendency to meet that need by exerting control over others. He was being offered opportunities for roles outside of his organisation and had a wife and teenage children who were used to a life that afforded a fair degree of comfort. Add to that the fact that he profiled as more risk averse than most, particularly under pressure, and it starts to become clear how his own needs and habits were contributing to this situation – whereas he, like most of us, saw the 'problem' as something that existed completely outside of him. Christoff's boss was at a very different stage in his life and career, with different priorities and pressures upon him. He was also less detail-conscious, more tolerant of ambiguity and had considerable appetite for risk. In other words: on a very different wavelength from Christoff.

- **The relationship between you and your boss.** Perhaps they trust you so much that – rightly or wrongly – they don't feel the need to give you more clarity. Perhaps they're afraid of offending you or patronising you if they're too clear. Perhaps they don't trust you enough. We'll look at trust in detail when we explore the next lesson 'Take due responsibility'.

When I asked Christoff to describe his approach to his boss, it was clear that his directness was creating a confrontational dynamic. The call for clarity sounded like a demand, even an ultimatum, rather than a request. What was lacking was a more adult-to-adult conversation that tabled Christoff's needs and desire to stay with the organisation while showing empathy with his boss's position.

- **Your boss's context.** Perhaps, as with Christoff's boss, there are external reasons why they can't be as clear as they'd like to be. Perhaps they're forbidden from sharing certain information, like at Apple where the shroud of secrecy over new products means bosses can't share certain things but accept that that means their staff will make some decisions that'll look 'bad' in hindsight – the payoff being the millions of dollars' worth of free advertising generated by the excitement that secrecy creates. Perhaps your boss is being influenced by their own boss's or peers' very different view of you or your relationship. Perhaps there are dynamics in your team that make it hard for them to be as clear as they might be otherwise. Perhaps the landscape is changing too quickly or the situation is too complex or ambiguous for them to gain sufficient clarity themselves.

Without sufficient clarity, it's going to be harder for us to deliver as well on what our bosses and other senior stakeholders want or need from us. It'll also be harder for us to fully commit to the endeavour and harder to galvanise others and hold them to account. So how should we get that clarity if it's not forthcoming? It's hard to give a single, simple answer. My hope is that by reflecting on the work you've done so far in this book and considering Christoff's situation and the four sources I've listed above, you'll see a way forward that suits your unique situation.

What did Christoff do? He took a step back, analysed what he and his boss were bringing to the situation, in terms of interpersonal style and the needs they had for themselves and for the business. He considered the stakeholders around them and what a good outcome and process would look like for them. Then he took these insights to his boss and negotiated a level of clarity and certainty that would allow him to relax for the next eighteen months while allowing the business the flexibility it needed during what was a challenging time for everyone. Last time I checked, he was still there and doing well.

Putting the Five-Phase Framework into practice

In case you'd like to create your own checklist here, I've left you some space to do so on the following pages.

Whether you do that or not, I'd encourage you to experiment with the Five-Phase Framework and use the space below to record the successes and challenges you've encountered when applying it to your own work and to your relationship with your boss and other senior stakeholders.

Ways in which the Five-Phase Framework has helped

....

....

....

....

Challenges I've faced when implementing the Five-Phase Framework

....

....

....

....

Your Five-Phase checklist

(This page is left blank for you create your own set of reminders should you wish to do so.)

Applying this lesson as a leader of others

If you lead people yourself, I'm hoping this lesson will have encouraged you to think about the degree of clarity you've been giving others. As we saw at the start, if you don't Establish a clear Direction with your people, you'll find it hard to Secure their Commitment and between you you'll find it hard to ascertain, let alone Build, the necessary Capacity to get the job done.

The three ARC Qualities have a role to play here, too. Clarity of purpose makes it easier to allocate responsibilities, and clear responsibilities increase people's commitment. Clarity makes it easier to be courageous in the face of adversity because it's far easier to push on through when you know where you're meant to be headed – ambiguity and uncertainty rob us of our momentum.

On the flipside, being clear with the people we lead isn't always easy: sometimes it requires us to draw on our values and those of the people we lead in order to find an authentic way forward; sometimes the path is obscured by a web of competing responsibilities; sometimes it takes courage to cut through the noise and be clear; sometimes it takes a combination of authenticity, responsibility and courage to admit to our staff that we're struggling to be clear with them because we're far from clear in our own minds.

So, if you have responsibility for leading others, I'd encourage you to use this Five-Phase model and the Seven Levels of Delegation explicitly with them. I'd invite you to challenge yourself to be as clear as you can be and challenge them to do the same.

In summary

Without clarity on the intended direction and criteria for success, it's hard to fully commit, to marshal the necessary resources to get the job done, and to measure progress. We've drawn on a Five-Phase Framework that helps you Engage the right people, Assess what's needed, Align your stakeholders, Progress that plan and Review your progress and ways of working.

If you've really tackled this lesson you'll be ready to use this approach in your own work and you'll know at any given time at which of the Seven Levels of Delegation you and your boss are operating.

• ● •

Taking stock

• ◉ •

> • What we've covered
>
> • What you've learned
>
> • How you'll put this into practice

YOU MIGHT BE ONE of those people who are reading this book from start to finish. You might be skipping parts, perhaps whole lessons, looking for the critical nuggets you feel are most relevant to you. Or perhaps you're bouncing back and forth, reading the book out of sequence, focusing on those lessons that feel most pertinent to your current situation.

Depending on your approach, the summary I'm about to provide of the first five lessons will serve a different purpose, as will the questions that follow.

Lesson 1: Have a vision of your own	We acknowledged that there are reasons not to bother having a vision and that creating one can be challenging, but that those reasons and challenges are far outweighed by the benefits: greater, more consistent motivation; enhanced resilience, job satisfaction and satisfaction with our lives in general; a focal point that can guide us through difficult times and decisions; a healthy, productive way of measuring our progress. If you used the tools I offered to help you with this lesson, you'll have a clear, compelling statement of intent that's been thoroughly tested and backed up with clear actions to get you started. You'll also have some allies to help you turn that vision into reality.

Lesson 2: Choose your leader wisely

In what has been without doubt the most contentious lesson in this book, I encouraged you to give serious thought to any situation where you're faced with a change in leadership. Sure, many of us feel we can't choose our leader, but the intention here is to encourage you to really do your homework – to get to know a potential new boss, sponsor or senior stakeholder before you commit to the relationship. At the very least, this puts you in a better position to clarify up front what you and they will need and how you'll need to adapt to create maximum value in the relationship – for you, for them, for all the people and organisations you are there to serve. If you've answered the various questions I've posed, then you'll have a clear picture of the kind of leader you're looking for and whether those above and around you at the moment are the right leaders for you.

Lesson 3: Challenge your assumptions

I asked "In what ways are you setting your leader up to disappoint you?" and introduced you to ways of examining your own attitude to and assumptions about relationships, the world and the very nature of leadership. Drawing on these, you had the opportunity to explore the expectations those attitudes and assumptions create in you and how those expectations may be aligned or misaligned with those of your boss(es). If you dug deep in that chapter, you'll have a different view of yourself, your bosses (past, present and future) and you'll have practical ideas for creating the optimal conditions for your relationships with the people leading you.

Lesson 4: **We get the** **leader we** **deserve**	The core question here was 'In what ways are you inadvertently derailing your boss?' This book is here to help you. At the same time, my intention is to challenge you to take responsibility for the things you can influence in the relationships with the people 'above' you – however flat your organisation or unofficial its hierarchy is. The questions you'll have asked yourself here will have got you thinking about the ways in which you're using the relationship(s) with your boss and others to get your fundamental needs met. You'll have considered, too, the less-than-optimal behaviours you demonstrate when you feel unable to get those needs met – and the ways those behaviours trigger or reinforce behaviours you'd rather not be seeing in your boss.
Lesson 5: **Seek clarity**	I asked 'How can you ever truly deliver if you don't know what they really want?' All too often, we make assumptions at the outset without clarifying our bosses' true needs, aspirations and concerns. We tend to take the explicit objectives and parameters they hand us without digging deeper into the implicit, unspoken needs and boundaries they have around the work we're doing. Too frequently, we get clarity at the start but forget to check back later on, so we miss changes in their priorities or the organisational ecosystem. To help with this, I introduced you to the Five-Phase Framework for ensuring clarity throughout: Engage, Assess, Align, Progress, Review. Then I asked you to take this framework, apply it and record the successes and challenges you encountered when doing so.

What are the key themes you're noticing so far in your relationship with your current boss (and with other senior stakeholders if you've been thinking about them, too)?

....

....

....

What are you noticing about the behaviour patterns and attitudes you bring to these relationships?

....

....

....

If you could change one thing about those behaviour patterns or attitudes that could make a significant positive difference to one or more of those relationships, what would it be, and why?

....

....

What 2-3 things could you start doing differently right away that would show you're making progress on your answer to the previous question?

....

....

....

● ● ●

6

Lesson 6:
Take due responsibility

● ● ●

- What's in it for you?

- What should (and shouldn't) you be taking responsibility for?

- Do your boss and others trust you enough to let you take responsibility?

- What do we really mean by 'trust', and how can you get more of it?

Why take on additional responsibility?

SOME PEOPLE DO so for selfish reasons, some out of generosity or a desire to contribute. You might even choose to do it for both. With additional responsibility comes increased opportunities for development and career progression – particularly in flatter organisations where progression can no longer only mean moving to the next rung in the official hierarchy. For those of us with an interest in acquiring power, authority and status, increased responsibility is a symbol of both. Taking responsibility also enables us to better support the people around and above us. Most people – leaders and otherwise – experience many of their responsibilities as a weight upon their shoulders. When we take some of that weight off them – as long as it's with their blessing – they're generally grateful. For you, that gratitude might be reward in itself, or it might be currency you'll exchange for something more tangible further down the line – some kind of favour or recognition in return for the credit you've already earned in that relationship.

Most leaders I've met feel they lack sufficient time to focus on the bigger, higher level challenges they should be addressing. They're trapped in a web of smaller responsibilities that are preventing them from 'leading at their level'[47]. Taking some of those responsibilities off of your boss frees them up to focus on activities that will deliver greater long-term value to the whole team, including you, and to your various stakeholders inside and outside the organisation.

> "Countless books have been written to describe the qualities and responsibilities of a leader, but democracy cannot survive unless followers also behave responsibly"
>
> Barber Conable, Jr
> Former President, World Bank[46]

People who fail to take due responsibility, or avoid it or manage their boundaries so much that they're unhelpful or obstructive, risk being seen as self-serving 'jobsworths'. Conversely, the kinds of people who really deliver value and thrive in (most) organisations are the ones who are proactive about seeking additional responsibility. There's a wealth of research showing that people who go beyond their job descriptions (engaging in what psychology calls Organisational Citizenship Behaviours) are more productive[48], get on better with their bosses[49], get better performance ratings[50] and tend to stay longer in their organisations[51] – four things that are almost certainly related! They also increase knowledge sharing[52]; contribute positively to the cohesion[53], performance[54] and profitability[55] of the groups and teams in which they're working and help improve the overall effectiveness of management throughout the organisation[56]. Unsurprisingly, by willingly and enthusiastically taking on additional responsibility, these people improve both the financial and non-financial performance of their organisations[57].

These proactive people are also responsible in the way they go about taking on those additional responsibilities. I've seen far too many middle managers suck up responsibility from below them while taking on increasing responsibility from above. As understandable as that is, it's also irresponsible: overloading ourselves ultimately leads to burn out, mistakes, letting people down, career derailment or all of the above. Hence the lesson here being to take *due* responsibility, not responsibility for everything we can get our hands on.

Responsibility for what?

That'll depend on your own seniority, experience and context. It'll also be influenced by the mind-set you have regarding your boss's role and responsibilities (which you can explore in Lesson 3 if you've not already done so). Your decisions regarding responsibility should also take into account your aspirations. Are you looking to take on a more senior role yourself or are you looking for work that's more inspiring, challenging, rewarding or interesting than the work you're currently doing? Are you looking to enhance your current standing in the organisation or protect what you've already accrued?

You'll want to factor all of those things in when answering that question "Responsibility for what?" When answering that question myself, I find it helpful to think in terms of Three Domains of Responsibility: personal, professional and societal. The latter two are most relevant here.

Some people look to the societal domain, seeking to make a more significant contribution locally, nationally or globally. That contribution might take any number of forms: socio-economic, for example, or physical, ecological, political, cultural, scientific or technological.

Others choose to focus on the professional domain when seeking opportunities for additional responsibility. Some of those look beyond their organisation, wondering how they can broaden their remit with regard to customers, clients or end users; investors, shareholders or owners; regulators, unions or the wider labour market; the media or stock market analysts; suppliers or strategic partners; their profession as a whole. Others focus within their organisation, taking on bigger projects, increased complexity and/or more staff; providing cover for colleagues on parental leave or taking secondments; focusing on a particular agenda such as people development, diversity, process improvement or innovation; becoming custodians of the organisation's culture or long-term future.

As one leader pointed out, though, whatever you're taking responsibility for make sure you're focusing on outcomes, not inputs. That's the difference between being someone who says "I did my bit; it's not my problem if we didn't get the result we were hoping for" and someone who is adding genuine value by taking responsibility for the result itself, even if that means going beyond their official remit, helping others with their own pieces of the puzzle and/or overcoming unforeseen obstacles.

Hopefully you've started coming up with ideas already, but what else could you be taking responsibility for?

Given that it's also irresponsible to overwhelm ourselves with responsibilities, what responsibilities should you ensure someone else takes care of (e.g. by delegating), so you can take these additional things on?

If you've been unhappy with your boss for nine months or more, what responsibility could you be taking to help them evolve into the kind of boss you'd value more?

All of these are potentially powerful ways to take on greater responsibility and deliver greater value in any number of spheres. Given that we're focusing on your relationship with your boss, though, one area that makes a huge difference is the extent to which individuals take responsibility for their leaders' success.

When talking about responsibility, I often refer to the Yamashita Principle: that leaders are held to account for the failures of their subordinates. We see it all the time: CEOs quitting or losing their jobs because something bad happened on their watch that they should have been aware of. I don't disagree with this idea, although it seemed totally out of control when one of my clients discovered he was facing potential prosecution for mistakes made by staff before he'd been given the job of coming in to tidy things up. However, I do believe responsibility needs to work both ways: in truly effective teams, the team members will also take responsibility for the success of their leader. The alternative is continuing to promote parent-child style relationships between leaders and their staff, which we know is unhelpful at best and at its worst is profoundly corrosive.

If you're reducing the burden of leadership rather than adding to it, then you're a genuine asset to the people above you. You're adding real value if you're acting as a buffer (but not a blocker) between your boss(es) and the smaller issues. They'll have more faith in you, you'll have greater influence *and* you'll be doing more for the organisation if you streamline the larger issues so they're easily digestible. The same is true if you take responsibility for aspects of their communication with other stakeholders, particularly if you're contextualising their messages without diluting them so they're easier for other people to truly understand. And you'll maintain the respect and support of the people around you if you do all this without becoming an obstructive, self-important gatekeeper[58].

There's also a role to play in ensuring our leaders are seen "in terms of their real strengths, values, achievements, and goals"[59], rather than letting outside forces create an erroneous or distorted image of our boss. I'm quoting Ira Chaleff here and it's easy to confuse his words with a call for sucking up to the boss. That's not what this is about. It's not about peddling PR or propaganda, it's about helping our bosses navigate some of the nightmares inherent in leadership. The more senior a leader becomes, the more they are subjected to the halo and horns effects and what's known in the trade as the 'fundamental attribution error'. Together, these hard-wired human biases cause the people around them to brand the leader a hero or a villain based on a single event or behaviour – often their earliest, most recent or most emotive experience of that leader – and to blame their failures on deep-rooted character flaws and their successes on happenstance or the actions of the people around them. The reality is usually a great deal more complex.

So I'd encourage you to take a moment now and consider what you and your team mates are doing to facilitate your boss's success in the organisation...

....

....

....

Of course, your boss might not deserve your efforts to help them succeed. They could be a narcissist or psychopath. It's unlikely, but it's possible. If you're unhappy with your boss, your first step, if you've not yet taken it, should be to work through Lessons 2, 3 and 4 – all of which encourage you to look at your own contributions to having a 'good' or 'bad' boss right now. If you've done that and you're still convinced they're a fundamentally bad person, then I believe you have the same four options I laid out when recommending you choose your boss wisely:

1. Escape – by moving to a different team, department or organisation

2. Find a way to change their behaviour – for example, through feedback, role-modelling, or other forms of direct or indirect influence

3. Find a way to replace or remove them – probably the riskiest option as it can leave them, you and others with a sense of betrayal that can prove fiendishly hard to shift

4. Change your attitude to the situation – without losing your authenticity or making unacceptable sacrifices on a moral, reputational or material level.

Options 2 and 3 require you to step up to an even greater responsibility – your responsibility to the greater good, to the wider organisation and to the other people this person leads and will lead in future. It's likely to be harder to take action, and it'll probably require a fair bit of courage. So we'll return to courage in Lesson 9.

What gets in the way of us taking responsibility?

I once spent a year coaching a senior team in an organisation that's something of a British institution. We usually provide at least two coaches per team and on one occasion my colleague and I arrived as usual a good 30 minutes before the session to give us time to set up the room. As usual, the security guard phoned Penny*, the PA who'd been asked to look after us. No answer. So he left a voicemail and we sat and waited. With our encouragement, he called her another couple of times. Finally, 25 minutes after we'd arrived and with just five minutes until the start of our session, she appeared to take us upstairs.

On the way to the room, we passed Penny's desk and her phone with its flashing red light, so I mentioned the voicemails.

"Oh," she said, waving dismissively at the phone. "No one's ever taught me how to use voicemail."

I don't know how you'd feel in my position, but I was simultaneously shocked, dismayed, irritated, amused and saddened by Penny's lack of proactivity. But fast-forward 45 minutes and we were faced with pretty much the same phenomenon when asking the senior team how they'd progressed with the list of actions they'd set themselves in our last session. This was a list of activities – ranked for importance and broken out across one-, three- and six-month timeframes – that the team had enthusiastically created and agreed were the things they needed to achieve if the team was to be successful. They weren't small things, abstract things or 'teamy' things; they were specific, meaty tasks they'd said were important to them and their stakeholders.

And since our previous meeting, not one of them had even looked at that list. Why? Because they didn't think it was particularly relevant. They'd

* Her name wasn't actually Penny.

created the list to fill the time, to give us all something to focus on in the hours we had together. As I stood there listening to them explain why none of them had taken responsibility for ensuring the activities on that list were actually relevant and the work we were doing was genuinely valuable, I felt the same mixture of emotions I'd felt with Penny: shock, dismay, irritation, amusement and sadness. Thankfully, those emotions gave way to curiosity, which prompted an interesting conversation that moved the coaching forward.

Contrast this with the approach taken by front line staff at HomeServe, the UK's leading provider of home emergency assistance and domestic repairs (see below).

Responsibility on the front line at HomeServe[60]

- An elderly ex-customer called long after her insurance policy had expired to say her boiler was broken. She'd paid for 10 years without claiming but her husband had died and she'd had to cut costs. The employee who took her call took her case to the company's daily CustomerFirst forum, which is open to all staff and was created to empower people to discuss ways of helping customers in unusual circumstances and challenging the way the business does things. As a result of the call handler bringing the case to the forum, the customer's boiler was fixed free of charge.

- A visiting plumber saved the life of a long-term customer who had collapsed at home, using skills he'd learned as a volunteer lifeguard. He then asked for the same training to be offered to all engineers so they could help if they ever found themselves in a similar situation. The company agreed that it was "the right thing to do". HomeServe has since trained a thousand of its directly employed engineers in basic life-saving skills, and continues to offer this training to all new recruits.

So, what was it that caused Penny and that senior team to fail to take responsibility for things that, on the surface, seem so simple? What is it that could get in the way of you taking on additional responsibility? For me, there are four sources of resistance, the same kinds of sources we saw when we looked at seeking clarity in Lesson 5:

- Your context

- You

- 'Them' – i.e. your boss or other people you're seeking to take responsibility from

- The relationship between you and them.

When your context is the problem

The fact that Penny and the senior team displayed similar failures to take responsibility, to be proactive, take hold of things and focus on creating maximum value in the areas they could influence, suggested the problem was a systemic one – something coded into the cultural fabric of their organisation. But it's not just their organisation that suffers from this malaise. I've seen its varied symptoms in a range of different organisations, even those that select the most driven intelligent people their labour markets have to offer. It's there, for instance, when I'm teaching leaders to take a less directive, coaching approach with their staff, one in which they encourage their people to think for themselves by asking high-value questions rather than spoon-feeding them answers. The leaders themselves agree that it's an approach that stimulates autonomy, growth and greater commitment on the part of the people they lead, but they worry that their people will reject the approach. The same problem is there when executives ask if we can get the next tier down to be more proactive, more strategic and less reliant on them to tell them what to do.

Of course, the widest, most deep-rooted context is the society in which we live. Even in less hierarchical cultures like the USA's and UK's, people are very quick to pass responsibility upwards. In my home country of Britain, for instance, it's one major contributor to our over-reliance on medical experts to manage our health, rather than owning that primary care ourselves. It's also there in the readiness of many nations' people to blame their governments for the divisions between different socioeconomic groups, rather than acknowledging how their own agendas and day-to-day behaviours contribute to those divisions.

Take a moment to identify five 'unspoken rules for success' in your organisation. These are the rules that nobody would ever say out loud, because they're embarrassing, shame-inducing or seem a little ridiculous, but that actually guide quite a lot of behaviour in the organisation. Then work out the ways each of those 'rules' encourages or discourages you from being proactive and/or taking additional responsibility.

What could you do differently to overcome those contextual barriers to taking responsibility?

....

....

....

....

....

....

When you're the problem

In the course of my work, I've come across five main reasons for people failing to take on additional responsibility, each of which can be working consciously or unconsciously, and each of which has nuances of its own. I've explored these in detail in *ARC Leadership*[61], which goes into greater depth on the topic of responsibility than is possible in this book, so I'll just touch on them briefly here:

1. "I can't do it" – usually because I think I'm too busy or under-resourced, or because I fear I lack the skills or intellectual capacity to make a good job of it

2. "I shouldn't do it" – either because taking on that responsibility would be seen as interfering or over-stepping a boundary, or because it'll cost me too much if I take it on

3. "Someone else will do it" – perhaps because it's more obviously their responsibility, or because they've no less reason to do it than I do. The most obvious candidates, of course, are the people above me in the hierarchy

4. "I don't want to do it" – because either I don't find it sufficiently interesting, I doubt it'll be worth my while, it's inconsistent with my beliefs about myself, or I believe the people I'd be helping don't deserve my help

5. "I can't decide right now" – I'm effectively paralysed by indecision, which could happen, for instance, if I'm working in a complicated matrix structure and struggling to work out exactly what to take responsibility for, or if my environment is so complex, ambiguous and constantly changing that it's hard to decide how best to *take on* a responsibility I'm keen to take.

When you think of the things you could be taking responsibility for, which of those five barriers resonate most?

What assumptions are you making in letting those barriers get in your way? How could you challenge or overcome those assumptions to expand your areas of responsibility?

It's well worth considering how work you've done previously in this book can help you here. Your vision and sense of who you are should help, as should your work considering your attitudes to your boss and the role they're 'meant' to play. Where questions of your own capacity, capability or bandwidth are concerned, getting clarity can help enormously – as can the topics we'll cover in Lesson 7. So, too, can mapping out your existing responsibilities and working out where else in the system around you those responsibilities could sit. For instance, is there something you could delegate to others to increase your spare capacity, so your boss feels more able to delegate something more interesting and/or more challenging to you?

Of course, there's always the possibility that you really *shouldn't* take on certain additional responsibilities. There could be a risk of being dragged into too much and becoming over-burdened. In some cases, in some relationships, you might also be exposing yourself to becoming the lightning rod or scapegoat when things go wrong. More than one person I've shared this lesson with has recalled that kind of experience, where a serious problem has arisen and their boss and/or senior commissioning stakeholder has stepped behind them or disappeared entirely, leaving them taking all the flak. Hence the title of this lesson is 'Take *due* responsibility'. Which brings us to our next two possibilities: where difficulties with responsibility are down to the boss, not you or the context, or where the problem lies in the relationship between you.

When they are the problem

Sometimes, it's not us and it's not the context in which we find ourselves, it's other people that are the root of the problem. That's why, in Lesson 2, we considered some of the overplayed strengths and counterproductive habits to watch out for when choosing whether to work for or align ourselves with a potential boss or other senior stakeholder.

If you've completed Lesson 4, you'll have explored how your own behaviours can inadvertently undermine your seniors' ability to deliver on your expectations, and you might remember us touching on three fundamental human needs:

- To feel significant

- To feel competent and in control

- To be liked.

Just as our needs – and the extent to which they're met or not met – drive our behaviours, our bosses' needs will affect their willingness to share responsibility and their approach to doing so, as will their habitual patterns of behaviour and their assumptions about us, themselves and the world around them. Add pressure and stress, and those needs and habits will become exaggerated, those assumptions more extreme and entrenched. This then has a knock-on effect on their approach to sharing responsibility.

Some common patterns we see under such circumstances, and even in less pressured times include:

- *Being distracted or stretched too thin:* bosses with this problem seem to quickly lose interest in the things they've delegated, shifting their attention to the next big thing. They may also tend to write you off if they think you've let them down, so it'll be harder to secure additional responsibilities following a mistake, perceived mistake, or if you fail to meet their standards.

- *Sucking up responsibility:* whether it's because they're over-confident, lacking in confidence or putting on a show of confidence, some leaders find it hard to resist taking it all. Some present as heroes, others as martyrs. Many eventually burn out. Some explode like supernovas, making huge high-profile mistakes that take their teams, departments or organisations with them. Some come to their end more quietly, like black holes, creating a vacuum where everyone around them is affected but no one can work out how they did it all so no one can pick up the pieces.

- *Hogging the sexy stuff:* most of us would be happy to rid ourselves of work we find boring, as long as we can be confident it'll be done well enough so there's little or no risk involved in someone else taking it off our hands. However, some bosses fail to consider the demoralising impact of delegating boring work they believe is beneath them. A few do consider this and do it anyway – sometimes as a display of power; sometimes because the company culture is one that promotes career progression as a means for rising stars to cascade the misery their superiors heaped on them.

- *Craving approval:* a boss who's struggling to get sufficient validation from the people around or above them will likely share responsibilities only when doing so serves their needs and makes them look good; they're less likely to consider your interests or needs and if the situation or their agenda changes, they're likely to snatch back those responsibilities or find ways to realign what you're doing for their own reputational gain.

- *Being afraid, isolated, insecure or perfectionistic:* whether it's because they find it hard to trust anyone, they feel utterly alone, they're obsessed with high standards, they're afraid of failure or that "they're only as good as their last job", or they're concerned about upsetting their superiors, the results are pretty much the same. These bosses will either withhold responsibility, smother you in scrutiny and control measures, or they'll abdicate rather than delegate so they can avoid being blamed for any mistakes or shortfalls.

- *Seeming vague and/or inconsistent:* they might be unclear in their own mind where the lines or boundaries of responsibility lie. Perhaps they're unsure of the options or other people's wishes or requirements where responsibility is concerned. Perhaps their views change daily as their own thoughts, feelings and environment fluctuate. If this is the case, I'd recommend focusing on Lesson 5 (seek clarity) if you haven't already done so.

- *Sharing reluctantly and begrudgingly:* bosses with this pattern will find it hard to say "no" if you ask for additional responsibility, but they may resent it and they'll find it hard to give you clear, honest feedback if your work doesn't live up to their expectations. If that resentment builds, they may start talking about you behind your back, which could harm your reputation, and – in extreme cases – they may deliberately or unconsciously sabotage your work.

I appreciate that my call (in Lesson 2) to choose your leader(s) wisely is somewhat contentious. However, if we *do* do our homework before agreeing to work for someone, we're less likely to end up with someone who regularly displays the patterns above. At the same time, we're all human, so one or more of those patterns is bound to crop up from time to time. Plus, of course, it's usually not just our direct bosses who are involved when we're looking to take on additional responsibility: there are other stakeholders, too, and each of those might fall into some of those same unhelpful patterns.

What patterns do you see in your boss (or others) that are making it harder for you to take on additional responsibility?

So how do we deal with these challenges?

Generally, I've found the best starting point is to empathise. This doesn't mean sympathising or condoning their behaviour, it means seeing the situation from their perspective. For example, if a leader or one of your other stakeholders is clinging onto responsibility, it could be because they feel isolated or they're afraid that handing over too much responsibility will make them look weak or incapable, reduce their authority or render them redundant because they'll be left with nothing to do. Or it could be because they're consciously or unconsciously hiding in those responsibilities so they have an excuse not to tackle harder topics where they feel less confident. It could be because they lack confidence in their ability to delegate or because they've been burned in the past. As with bosses who aren't being sufficiently clear, there may be contextual factors at play, too: pressure from above or outside the organisation, a difficult relationship with their peers or another member of your team, and so on.

We all have an inbuilt need to be understood. Bosses and other stakeholders who feel we understand their hesitation to share responsibility are far more likely to relax their grip. Those who see our efforts to take on additional responsibilities as a threat – either because we're taking something precious from them or because we're taking on work we might prioritise over the things we're doing for them – are more likely to seek to neutralise that threat.

In empathising with those who are making it harder for us to take on additional responsibility, we're starting to work on the relationship between us. So that's where we'll turn next.

When the relationship is the problem

There's one single factor that has a disproportionate influence on how willing our bosses, peers and other stakeholders are to accept our efforts to take on additional responsibilities. That same factor applies whether we're explicitly taking responsibility from those people or simply increasing the scope and/or diversity of our responsibilities. That factor is trust. Critically, though, while it may be a single factor, it's not a simple factor.

In *ARC Leadership*[62], I offered a seven-factor research-based framework for looking at trust – seven levers that, if you and I were working together, would determine how much you'd be willing to trust me. As I've continued to use that model with clients, it's been helpful to highlight two additional levers, creating the framework you see below. For the sake of simplicity, the statements in the image are binary: they ask for 'yes' or 'no' answers. In reality, each question should be preceded with "How much...?" or "To what extent...?"'

The two outer rings show us that trust is not just about you and me. It's also about the company we keep and the organisational culture in which we exist. If you don't trust my people – the friends, allies and the staff I'm relying on to get stuff done – then it's a lot harder for you to trust me. If we're working in an organisation where most people trust each other, it'll obviously be easier for you to trust me and me to trust you. If we're working in an organisation with a high blame culture, where people lose their jobs in an instant, then it'll be so much harder for us to trust each other. Sure, once we *do* trust each other, we're likely to value our relationship enormously. But, it'll be much harder for us to get to that point in the first place.

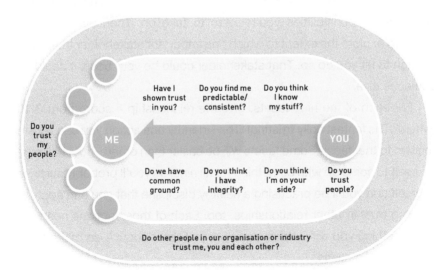

Saying that our bosses and other senior stakeholders need to trust us if they are going to give us additional responsibility clearly isn't anything new. What's helpful, though, is having a framework like the one above to help us work out how much those people trust us, and *in what ways* they trust us.

Assessing our relationships with our bosses – or other important stakeholders – on all nine of these facets offers far greater insight into how we can increase the levels of trust in the relationship. It tells us what levers we'll need to pull to secure or enhance their faith in us. It draws our attention, for instance, to the fact that most leaders feel somewhat isolated and exposed, so showing them that we're on their side goes a long way – particularly given the prevalence of that Yamashita principle, which suggests our bosses will be hung out to dry if we mess up, but offers no promise of reciprocation. Similarly, when we take on new responsibilities, it can be easy for our existing stakeholders to assume that'll mean we'll be reprioritising or deprioritising something we're currently doing for them. Whether we are or not, it's helpful to consciously consider what action we'll need to take to maintain their trust, for instance by showing them we're still on their side.

Bearing all this in mind, I'd encourage you to think about the additional responsibilities you're keen to take on. Then use the table below to explore the extent to which one important stakeholder trusts you enough to let you do so. That stakeholder could be your boss; it could be someone else.

For each of the nine facets, give the relationship a score from 0-10 (where 10 is fantastically trusting). Then identify one action you can take in relation to that facet. Some facets will be easier than others, but challenge yourself to come up with something for all nine, as you'll probably surprise yourself and you'll be practising a healthy discipline that you can apply to building trust in other relationships, too. Each of those actions needs to be something you will actually do – not just think about – so make them tangible and realistic.

The extent to which they believe...	Trust score (0-10)	One action I can take to increase or respond effectively to that trust score
People in general can be trusted		
I have the knowledge and skills to do a good job		
I'm on their side, looking out for them and will take a hit for them (rather than putting my own needs or success ahead of theirs)		
I'll keep my word and keep their secrets[63]		
I'm predictable and consistent in my approach		
We have important things in common		
I've shown that I trust them (through actions, not just words)		
They can trust my friends, allies, confidants and the people I rely on to get things done		

The extent to which they believe...	Trust score (0-10)	One action I can take to increase or respond effectively to that trust score
The people around us (in this department, organisation, industry or profession) trust us and each other		
The overall extent to which they trust me (total score, out of 90):		

If you've worked through each of the nine facets, you'll have some concrete actions you can use to build trust in at least one important relationship. I'd recommend bookmarking this page so you can come back to it and reuse it for other relationships – whether those relationships are with other senior people in your organisation, with peers, with staff or with stakeholders outside the organisation.

One question that often comes up, at this point is...

"How do I get someone's trust back if I think I've lost it?"

The answer isn't a simple one. The research on recovering trust shows that whatever action we take we should include some kind of apology. The type of apology that will be most effective in a given situation depends both on the nature of the breach and the kind of person you're apologising to.

So the first step – whether you're building in an apology or not – is to identify which of the nine facets has (or have) been affected. Each is likely to dictate a different course of action. For instance, if the breach is around competence – i.e. that you or those who work for you have made a mistake that gives your boss the sense that you're less capable than they thought you were – then you'll need to do something to show that you've learned from the mistake and have taken steps to ensure it won't happen again. Personally, I'd say that's a bare minimum: to really recover the trust, you'll also need to demonstrate that you've used this as an opportunity to take your competence in that area (or your team's competence, if that's at fault) to a whole new level.

This speaks to something I believe is core to dealing with challenges in relationships: always seek to leave the relationship *better* than it was before. If their trust score in one area was 7 and something you've done has knocked it down to a 2, don't resign yourself to damage limitation. Don't aim to get back to a 'slightly worse than before but manageable' score of 5. Don't even settle for that familiar 7. Aim for 8 or 9. In doing so, we're turning a threat into an opportunity, rather than simply seeking to neutralise the threat.

If you are intending to apologise, you'd be advised to attend to these five core features that the research suggests are key to any successful apology[64]:

1. Express regret, never following "sorry" with "but…"

2. Explain and take responsibility for the actions that led to the breach

3. Offer some kind of compensation

4. Make a commitment to reducing the chances of any further breach of trust

5. Seek forgiveness.

Where the first of those five features is concerned, it's critical to look and sound sincere and genuinely sad about the breach. It's hard to imagine anyone thinking that seeming happy about the breach could increase the other person's trust, but research with apologetic CEOs suggests even a neutral expression will cause trust to erode further when we're apologising[65].

Different people and different cultures will respond differently to different expressions of regret[66]. For instance, people with a strong relationship focus will respond better if you share your understanding of the emotional impact the breach has (or might have had) on them. Whereas people who feel a strong affinity for a social group or the organisation as a whole – or who come from a more collectivist culture – will appreciate *your* appreciation of the impact the breach has had on the collective, its rules, its customs or its ways of working. The key, really, is to base your expression of regret on an understanding of what is important to *them* regarding the breach, not on what is important to you.

The second ingredient in our list, explaining and taking responsibility, is an interesting one from a psychological perspective. On one hand, the explanation helps the other party to empathise with us, to see that they might have acted similarly in the same situation. Their natural tendency as human beings is to blame others' transgressions, failures and mistakes on character flaws, underestimating the impact of situational variables on behaviour. Explaining the sequence of events helps counter that bias and reduces the chances that they'll put the breach down to some fundamental flaw in our character. On the other hand, if we take *insufficient* personal responsibility, they're less likely to believe we're truly sorry *and* less likely to believe we'll be able to prevent the breach happening again – which, of course, is another of the five features of a successful apology. This is because dodging responsibility by blaming situational variables sends signals that we lack the *competence* to remain trustworthy in those kinds of situations and/or that we're *unpredictable* in our ability to do so – either of which reduces the extent to which they should trust us in future.

Where compensation is concerned, it's important again to be attentive to what has value to the other party: some people will prefer concrete, perhaps financial, restitution. Others will want something more relational or symbolic like a public apology or social favour.

One final note on apologies: even people on the *receiving* end of apologies tend to overestimate the extent to which an apology will make up for a breach of trust[67]. So always be looking for what else you can do to bring trust back into the relationship.

Applying this lesson as a leader of others

Ultimately, if the people you lead don't take due responsibility – or you refuse to give it to them – then you're going to find it harder to succeed as their boss. At the same time, if you hand them responsibility without giving them due clarity (covered in Lesson 5) or checking they've sufficient capacity (covered in Lesson 7), then they might well disappoint you. So I imagine this lesson will have provoked a number of questions regarding your relationships with the people you lead.

A useful starting point to help you challenge your existing allocation of responsibilities would be to get a pad of post-it notes and on each post-it write one of the things for which you're currently responsible. Keep going until you've run out of things to write, but be wary of overwhelming yourself by getting too granular and remember to include things that typically go unmentioned (like team culture) or are more about relationships than ticking task boxes (like understanding and attending to the needs of a particular stakeholder).

Then, on separate post-it notes, ideally of a different colour, write your own name and the names of anyone reporting into you – including any matrixed reporting lines. Lay these post-its out in front of you, placing the one with your own name on it furthest away from you, just out of reach. Now challenge yourself to allocate each of the activities to different people by moving the post-its around. The key criteria for allocation should be the extent to which that activity will engage and safely stretch that individual in a manner that will help them thrive. Their current workload should not be a factor at this point and allocating an activity to yourself should always be the last resort.

Their capacity to take on those activities will obviously be a matter for discussion, and could involve them doing a similar activity for themselves, or you running a similar exercise as a team. Of course, whether you're prepared to hand these people any of your existing responsibilities will depend on how much you trust them and the extent to which you tend to fall foul of the patterns outlined on page 143. So I'd recommend reviewing those and completing your own version of the trust table on page 149 before you take these reallocations to your people. You and they will also benefit from discussing the content of Lesson 5 ('Seek clarity') to smoothen the transition with anything you're delegating to them.

In summary

We looked at the many personal benefits of taking due responsibility including development, career progression, status, power and the accumulation of others' trust, respect and gratitude. We touched on benefits to your team and organisation like enhanced performance, productivity, profitability and team cohesion.

You'll have decided what it is you could (and shouldn't) be taking responsibility for. You'll have seen the patterns in your reasons for sometimes dodging responsibility. You'll have identified reasons your boss might be reluctant to give you responsibility and you'll know how much they trust you, why and what you can do about it.

● ● ●

Lesson 7: Continually build your capacity

- Why continual growth is critical to retaining and increasing your value

- What skills, knowledge and resources will you need to develop to stay ahead of the game?

- What role are the processes and structures around you playing in enhancing or limiting your capacity to deliver?

- What contribution will you need to make to building the capacity of others?

IMAGINE YOU OWN A CAMEL – one hump or two, it's up to you.

You've taken that camel on many trips across the desert and it's done pretty well with 300kg of weight on its back. One day, you decide to take an extra 150kg. The trip is the same in all other respects.

The camel collapses a third of the way to your destination. Whipping it repeatedly doesn't appear to help. Shouting, stroking and soothing words have no effect either. What on earth is wrong with your camel?

Your capacity to do your job depends on a number of things:

- Your **knowledge and skills** – what some call 'capabilities' – and those of the people around you

- The **resources** available to you

- The **processes** you use and encounter that enable or inhibit your performance

- The organisational **structures** within which you're working.

> A 1% improvement on your current performance, applied every day for a year, multiplies your performance by 37.78
>
> Over the same year, a 1% decline per day reduces your performance to less than 3% of its current levels
>
> With the pace of change constantly increasing, if you're not improving, then relative to the world around you, you're in decline

Arguably, your camel fell short on all four. It was pushed too far beyond its current capabilities and it lacked sufficient resources to offset that stretch. In addition, it was working within a disablingly hierarchical structure that lacked the processes required to monitor its escalating workload and/ or gradually build its capacity to carry increasingly heavy loads. After all, a well-managed 1% daily increase in workload could potentially have increased its weight-bearing capacity by the required 150kg in less than two months.

Whether or not you've adopted Lesson 6 ('Take due responsibility'), the chances are your workload will be increasing and your job will be getting harder not easier. Unless you're operating at well below your potential, taking on additional responsibility without increasing your capacity is unsustainable and probably irresponsible. As one partner in a professional services firm said to me, most people – including our bosses – will treat us as though we're always operating at a maximum of 80-90% of our true capacity, so they'll feel free to add another few kilos to our load with little or no forewarning. However, few of us have factored this in when managing our workload, so we tend to operate at 90-100%.

Continually building our capacity goes beyond maintaining a sufficiently steep learning curve to stay ahead of the game when it comes to enhancing our knowledge and skills[68], particularly as the world grows increasingly volatile, uncertain, complex and ambiguous. So, in this lesson, we'll also look at ways to ensure you've the right resources, processes and structures in place to enable you to thrive.

Knowledge and skills / 'capabilities'

As individuals, it's important to continually work on increasing our subject matter expertise *without* becoming a slave to it. Critically, we need to evolve the very focus of that subject matter expertise so it's matching the pace of change in our professions and operating environments, and keeping up with our own progress up the career ladder. Every promotion must bring with it a recalibration to ensure you're 'leading at your level'[69]. Trying to technically outperform people at the level below us in the hierarchy will limit our ability to step up to higher levels of responsibility. Sure, in some organisations with a highly technical focus, there's an expectation that at least some of the top dogs are the ultimate subject matter experts who can resolve the technical problems that baffle their juniors. However, these are typically specialist roles and the more time those senior figures spend on individual technical problems, the less time they're spending on the higher level challenges their organisations are facing.

The same is true of skills: each level in any hierarchy requires a different set of skills from the levels below and above it. So each promotion requires a certain amount of unlearning of old habits, mind-sets and ways of viewing the world and our place in it – which takes us back to Lesson 3 ('Challenge your assumptions'). As we progress, the challenge is to acknowledge and accept this need to evolve – not just intellectually but emotionally – so we can actually make the behavioural and attitudinal changes required, rather than simply paying them lip service. And the challenge becomes to ensure that the level below us has the right combination of knowledge and skills to enable us to step up.

The skills themselves vary, of course, but they're generally fairly easily divided into skills demanding cognitive intelligence and those that demand emotional intelligence. The former include problem solving, planning, lateral thinking and strategic analysis. The latter include empathy, influence, team working, relationship building, adaptability, resilience and the ability to manage one's emotions. Decision-making straddles both domains: plenty of research shows that we make our decisions using our emotions then justify them with data after the fact, and that we actually struggle to make decisions at all if the emotion centres of our brain are damaged or disabled.

It's important to acknowledge here the difference between 'horizontal' learning and 'vertical' development. The former is essentially expanding your current territory when it comes to knowledge and skills. For example, if you worked in Human Resources, you could take a course in an HR topic you've not previously covered, or even add 'basic finance' to your CV. Both would expand your existing domains of knowledge, essentially "adding more apps"[70] to your current repertoire.

Vertical development is an upgrade to your entire operating system. It's a transformational shift in mind-set equivalent to the shift we see in a child as they suddenly develop the ability to see the world from other people's perspectives, so that they no longer think they can hide simply by closing their eyes. The different task and relationship mind-sets in Lesson 3 are examples of this vertical development and there's a growing literature on the topic if you'd like to explore it further[71]. Vertical development can be informed by knowledge *to some extent* – exploring that literature will help – and there are certain skills we can co-opt from others who are operating at 'the next level up'. A true shift, though, requires us to shed certain attitudes and beliefs that bind us to existing ways of thinking. We'll return to this idea towards the end of this lesson. For now…

What knowledge and/or skills do you think you should further develop to enable you to take on more responsibility and/or deliver greater value in your role?

....

....

....

What knowledge and/or skills could the people around or below you develop to enable them and you to take another step up?

....

....

....

To what extent do you have sufficient *diversity* of skills, knowledge and perspectives around you?

....

....

....

Importantly, do not wait for formal performance reviews to ask these questions. We need to "hunt feedback"[72], not wait for it to come wandering past our noses. If we wait for the annual or six-monthly appraisal, the feedback almost always comes too late. People have already made decisions about us and our future. Two useful things to remember when it comes to feedback, if you're not already thinking about them:

- There's been a big movement in the past few years calling for people to focus only on strengths when giving, seeking and acting on feedback. It is misguided and lacks a strong evidence base. Focus on making the most of your strengths, yes, but if we fail to attend to the weaknesses that are holding us back or negatively impacting on others, then they will continue to hold us back and negatively impact on others. If you'd like to explore this topic further, you'll find a link to an article in the references at the back of this book[73].

- We only get high-quality, honest feedback if other people feel they *can* give it to us. Yes, I know it sounds obvious, but the extent to which they feel able to give honest feedback will depend on a combination of their personality and their past experience of giving feedback to other people (in your organisation and other organisations). It'll also depend on their relationship with you, which will include their observations of your reactions to feedback and the extent to which you've turned past feedback into action. The first factor is out of your control. The second you can influence to some extent, but your impact will probably be minimal so you'll need to adapt your approach to work around it. The third factor is largely down to you.

Resources

There are probably as many different types of resource as there are different types of organisation. The most obvious and applicable across contexts are time, money, information and people (including their skills and knowledge, but sometimes just sheer numbers and force of will). And then, of course, there are the buildings, furnishings, machines and all the other physical objects that enable you, your team and your organisation to function.

Most, if not all, of the people I've worked with over the years feel under-resourced. The majority believe they lack sufficient time to get everything done. Many complain of being under-staffed and/or having budgets that aren't fit for purpose. Most of them find their headcount and budgets are shrinking year on year. As far as I can work out, this is the norm. It's also hard to believe it will ever stop being the norm. Capitalist consumerism is the dominant force driving most organisations. It's a force that venerates growth above all else and that demands that quality and profitability are always going up, and costs and delivery times are always coming down. "More, better, faster and for less"[74] is the mantra of most 21st-Century organisations – whether it's stated explicitly or not – and it's what their customers, clients and end users are clamouring for. This challenge is fuelled at a global level: our population and expectations are increasing but we're using up the available resources quicker than Nature can replenish them.

So, it seems to me that the clever people – the people who'll deliver *real* value without driving themselves or those around them to an early grave – will be the people who can jump off the hamster wheel of seeking ever-smaller efficiency savings and create a genuine step-change in how things are done.

Automation is helping in some regards, albeit while generating a fair amount of concern that efficiency savings will cause more harm than good. Another option is to get smarter about the distribution of responsibilities across the resources that *are* available. At an individual level, this could mean carving out time to step back from the day-to-day urgent (or seemingly urgent) activities to think more creatively or strategically. At a shop-floor level, my friend Mark works for a company in the USA that streamlines workforce planning for organisations like Wal-Mart, enabling them to reduce time wasted between (and within) the various repetitive tasks their people conduct on a daily basis.

At more senior levels in organisations, teams have mapped their combined responsibilities and critiqued the current distribution in pursuit of something better – and often 'better' includes pushing some responsibilities down the hierarchy to places where they become development opportunities rather than burdens.

A third way to deal with the resources challenge is to actively seek to *build* resources – to grow them, rather than accepting what we currently have or allowing someone else to take them away from us. We can do this by persuading others to give us more, but that's often a zero-sum game as those resources will typically be taken from elsewhere in the organisation. That might be fine if, by doing so, the organisation is investing the resource in a place that delivers greater value overall. However, it's an approach that's often rooted in selfishness, silo-thinking and political game-playing – none of which are in the best interests of the whole system. The alternative is a less competitive, more collaborative approach to building resources. Upskilling staff so each individual becomes a bigger resource; borrowing unused space from other organisations; sharing physical resources with neighbours; reusing, repurposing or recycling items that others have discarded or mothballed before they've delivered their full value; crowd-sourcing labour, funding or creativity... All of these are the beginnings of ideas that can help us increase the resources we have available to us.

What new, creative ideas do you have for increasing or getting more from the resources you and your boss have available to you? *(The wilder your initial thinking here, the better. It's in the most outrageous initial ideas that we find the beginnings of truly creative, yet practical, solutions. We just need the creativity to come first, then the practicality second.)*

Processes

Lesson 5 ('Seek clarity') focuses very much on a process you can use with the people who lead you. There are a host of other processes that'll enhance or reduce your capacity to deliver, to get results for you and for your boss. Some will be processes you use yourself, to manage your workload. Others will be processes you use with your boss, colleagues and/or the people you lead. The ones I've noticed making a real difference are those that deal with the following topics (you'll find resources for some of them at www.leaderspace.com):

Communication	When it comes to streamlining and managing written communication, too few people and teams consider alternatives to email like threaded discussions, instant messaging and cloud-based tools like Slack. Similarly, too few have established protocols for using different forms of written communication – who to 'cc', when to use WhatsApp versus email, when it is and isn't acceptable to email out of office hours, and so on. Where verbal communication is concerned, many high-performing teams use simultaneous text in combination with video-conferencing. They've also often adopted simple but sophisticated techniques to manage meetings, to balance structure with adaptability, to hear from everyone not just those who speak fastest or loudest, and focus as much on listening to each other as on tabling pre-baked points of view. They'll also attend to each other's different communication preferences when communicating verbally and in writing, perhaps aided by personality frameworks like the MBTI[75].

Information and knowledge management	I learned early through my work in forensic psychology that it's the ability to turn information into genuine intelligence that is key – for example, the *information* held prior to the 9/11 attacks in New York was sufficient to prevent those attacks happening, but the various agencies holding that information weren't sufficiently well connected with each other to join the dots. A critical feature here will be how you stay current in your understanding of the team, the organisation, its operating environment and the needs of its customers, clients or end users. This is a key issue even for some of the most senior people I've coached in organisations. Indeed, you could argue that the more senior you get, the more moving parts there are around you and the harder it gets to keep track of them.
Planning	Whether you're a natural planner or not, if you're working with a large group of people and/or your work is complex, failing to plan is a really bad idea. As some of my colleagues are fond of saying "Remember the Six Ps: Prior Planning and Preparation Prevents Poor Performance"[76].
Client / customer / stakeholder relationship management	Some teams do this very consciously, some do it very well and some even manage both. Many rely on memory and impulse. Too many have no way of knowing whether their colleagues have spoken to the team's clients, customers or stakeholders, or what was said, and find themselves tripping over each other and embarrassing the team as a whole.

Decision-making	Most of the teams I've worked with have little or no agreed process for making decisions. All too often, decisions seem to be made by accident or by the loudest or most persistent person in the room. When working with teams, I'll often introduce them to the difference between 'debate' and true 'dialogue'[77] and we'll talk about the role of unconscious bias in decision-making. I'll also sometimes reference the 'zig zag' decision-making model[78] (another MBTI tool).
Accountability	How do you keep track of who is accountable for what, when they're meant to do it by and what will happen if they don't? Too many teams and their leaders leave results far too much to chance, or prioritise being nice over being clear and fair, or fume quietly when people fail to deliver then hammer them at the end of the year. Others hold people to account for *activities* rather than *outcomes*, which can reduce the extent to which people take genuine responsibility for the success of the shared endeavour – they can easily say "I did my bit; it's not my fault if it didn't work out".
Conflict management	My colleagues and I frequently find ourselves helping individuals and teams enhance their ability to work with conflict. Done well, conflict is an essential feature of high-performing teams, but it's easy to default to a culture of false harmony and conflict-avoidance. Some people and teams do repeatedly dip their toes into conflict, but they withdraw too soon rather than sticking with it and working through to a mutually agreeable resolution.

Harnessing diversity

Diversity is by its very nature disruptive. Managed poorly, that disruption has a negative impact, which means it's potentially worse than having no diversity at all. Managed well, diversity reduces risks and enhances creativity and performance. Managing it well means managing all of the above processes well, while remembering to encourage, accommodate and harness the various diverse perspectives involved – perspectives that could come from working in different locations; coming from different faiths, ethnic groups, generations, departments or previous organisations; or favouring different working styles.

What opportunities do you see for enhancing the processes in and around your team, to increase your collective capacity to deliver?

....

....

....

How effectively do you and your boss manage each of these processes in your own relationship? How might you enhance those that aren't delivering as much value as they could be?

....

....

....

Structures

The extent to which you can influence the structure around you will depend on your own seniority in the organisation. However, wherever you sit in the hierarchy, you can choose to get better at noticing and responding to the effects of that structure on the behaviours and performance of those around you.

There's an awful lot to be said about the impact of different team and organisational structures, so my intention is to explore this topic more fully in a future book, focusing on teams as a whole. At the team level, for example, a common structure is the 'hub and spoke', where the leader is at the centre and each team member primarily only communicates with the leader, who makes all the major decisions. The effectiveness of this structure depends entirely on the context in which the team is operating, the team's purpose and the nature of its various tasks. However, the hub and spoke structure often happens by default, rather than by choice: either because of the team leader's preferences, the dominant team members' preferences, or a combination of the two.

At an organisational level, structures vary based on features like span of control, the number of rungs on the ladder of hierarchy and degrees of centralisation and specialisation. Most taxonomies will differentiate between the following four structures[79]:

- **Functional**, where people are primarily aligned according to their job functions (marketing, sales, finance, etc.). This structure is highly scalable and provides staff with clear career paths, but is driven by internal priorities and can create competition between the different functions and provoke clashes between different subcultures.

- **Divisional**, where people are primarily aligned to a particular product, market or geography (e.g. 'food', 'beverages' and 'furniture'; 'business-to-business' and 'business-to-customer'; 'Europe', 'Asia' and 'Africa'). These models are often more customer-focused, offering faster, more tailored services, and if one division fails the others are (usually) protected, but generally create duplication of effort and involve a tension between local autonomy and centralised control.

- **Process-based**, where each person or team handles a particular portion of the product or customer lifecycle (for example, with aircraft engines: 'design', 'sales', 'tailoring', 'installation' and 'aftercare'). This structure is usually quick and adaptable, but can lead to bottlenecks, particularly if the interdependencies between each stage in the process (and hence each team) aren't managed effectively.

- **Matrixed**, which is usually a combination of the functional and divisional structures, and involves people having at least two reporting lines. For instance, I could be a Financial Controller working in Paris for a multinational, reporting to the company's Global Finance Director and to the Managing Director of the French operation. The potential benefits are flexibility, more informed decision-making and more efficient use of resources. The potential downsides are complexity, confusion and the need to balance the priorities of two bosses with very different agendas.

In what ways is the structure in and around your team helping you to do your job?

....

....

....

....

....

....

....

In what ways is the structure in and around your team a hindrance to your effectiveness? What can you do to change that?

....

....

....

....

....

....

....

....

The bigger picture

If you're delivering on this lesson, you'll be constantly – or at least frequently – developing your own capacity. You'll be building your knowledge and skills; ensuring you and your boss have the resources you need; staying sufficiently fit, fresh and healthy; refining your own processes and the processes around you; and finding ways to influence and/or work with the prevailing structure in order to deliver exceptional results.

If you're really keen, though, and really adding value, you'll be contributing in a broader way. You'll be building capacity amongst your peers, your support network and across the wider organisation. If you're really looking to add value and to stretch yourself into broader spheres of responsibility, you'll also be looking to build capacity in your wider operating environment – like my friend Jeff, who helped drive educational standards at the universities that feed his profession.

Where in the system are you building capacity? *(If you created a map of your boss's world at the end of Lesson 4, on **page 94**, you might find that a good place to head for inspiration. If you didn't, then you'll find it helps here to sketch a map of the system around you.)*

....

....

....

....

....

....

....

What else could you be doing to build capacity and where could you be doing it?

....

....

....

....

....

....

....

What capacity is your boss struggling to create for themselves? What can you do to change the way they're looking at that challenge?

....

....

....

....

....

....

....

Thinking in terms of skills, knowledge, resources, processes and structures: what assumptions are you making about your current capacity and capacity-building in general? How can you challenge these assumptions to make a step-change in the way you approach questions of capacity?

....

....

....

....

....

....

....

Applying this lesson as a leader of others

The questions I've posed throughout this lesson ask you to look beyond your own capacity. You'll have considered the enabling and inhibiting factors presented by your peers and the people you lead – in terms of their knowledge and skills, as well as the resources you share, the processes that govern the ways you work together and the structures within which you operate.

When considering the capacity you need to build in the people that follow you, you'll want to attend to ensuring any capacity-building is aligned with the team's and organisation's chosen direction. You'll need to secure your people's commitment to building that additional capacity, not least because it'll likely require effort and courage on their part. You're more likely to get that commitment if building the capacity you're looking for helps them make progress in the personal directions they've chosen, i.e. if it's aligned with the individual visions you've encouraged them to create in response to Lesson 1 ('Have a vision of your own').

You'll also need to secure the commitment of key stakeholders to building capacity among your people: developing them could require budgetary sign-off, additional tolerance of risk or underperformance as your people go through a period of stretch, or your staff taking on greater responsibility than your stakeholders might initially be prepared to tolerate.

I'd encourage you to discuss all of these challenges with the people you lead, and to explore the role of existing skills, knowledge, resources, processes and structures in enabling and inhibiting their current and future performance.

In summary

Unless you continually build your capacity, you'll be left behind as the world moves on around you. Capacity-building is about more than increasing your knowledge and skills. It requires attending to your vertical development – a shift in mind-set to increasingly sophisticated ways of seeing the world. It's about marshalling and managing resources; designing and evolving optimal processes; and utilising or changing the structures in which we operate to get results. Making a real difference when it comes to capacity will also mean building capacity elsewhere in the system, so you're genuinely contributing not just to your own success but to the success of others.

If you've given thought to the questions I've offered, you'll have a clear view of the capacity you need to build in yourself and in others. You'll also have ideas for process improvements and for working more effectively with the structures in which you operate.

• ● •

8

Lesson 8: Secure and maintain commitment

• ● •

- How your commitment will have a tangible impact on your performance

- What is it, exactly, that you should be committing to?

- Who else's commitment is critical to your success?

- How to manage your own commitment and that of your boss and key stakeholders

THE THREE CORE DISCIPLINES have been a common thread

throughout this book. Lesson 1 ('Have a vision of your own') focuses on you having your own individual *direction*. Lesson 2 ('Choose your leader wisely') considers, among other things, the importance of ensuring your leader's chosen direction is aligned with your own. Lesson 5 ('Seek clarity') helps ensure you and your boss have mutual clarity on the direction you're meant to be headed. Lesson 7 ('Continually build your capacity'), attends to your *capacity* to head in that direction. In this lesson, we're focusing on commitment. Not just your commitment, but the importance of managing your boss's commitment and that of your shared stakeholders. We'll look at understanding your own commitment and theirs, and what you can do to secure greater commitment and to recapture it when it's waning.

Your commitment *will* naturally wax and wane over the course of a year, a month, a week, and even a day. As Gallup's statistics (see below) suggest, that waxing and waning will have a tangible impact on your productivity, safety and desire to stay – at your desk, in your job, with your current boss and with  your current organisation. It'll affect your willingness to go the extra mile and take on responsibilities outside your job description and it'll have a knock-on effect for your ability to deliver on each of the other lessons in this book. Your commitment will affect your relationships with bosses, colleagues, staff and customers, which will contribute to the waxing and waning of their commitment to you and the organisation.

When you're truly committed you are:

- 24-59% less likely to quit

- 17% more productive

- Likely to be rated at least 10% higher by your customers

- 70% less likely to get injured

- 28% less likely to be tempted to steal from your employer

- Potentially contributing 21% more to profitability

- Distinguishing yourself from the 24% of people who are actively disengaged, by joining the minority 13% who are actively engaged with their work.

Gallup[80]

Similarly, if your boss's commitment fades it'll make life harder for you – and everyone else they lead. It'll make it harder to get high-quality feedback and career development. It'll likely reduce the chances that they'll advocate for you and the work you're doing, that they'll defend you when you're under fire or push things through for you when you hit a seemingly immovable obstacle.

It's also in both your interests to contribute to securing and maintaining the commitment of your shared stakeholders, including any of your colleagues who also report into the same boss. Your success and your boss's success will probably be heavily dependent on all of those stakeholders pulling in the same direction, rather than slowing things down or actively working against you.

Finally, if you're a leader in your own right then your commitment will also be influenced by (and influence) the commitment of the people you lead. As with the other lessons, we'll return to your potential use of this lesson with the people you lead at the end of the chapter.

Commitment to what?

Even in an organisation with a simple, stable, non-matrixed line-management structure, there are *at least* six things to which you (and others) might choose to commit. There'll be others too, of course, specific to you and your environment. Plus, each of the various agendas will vary in scale and scope, the degree to which it is explicitly and clearly articulated, and the extent to which it focuses on the long-term versus today and the coming weeks and months.

1. Your own vision for yourself

2. Your boss or bosses' chosen direction(s)

3. The team you're part of, as a member not the leader

4. The team(s) you lead, if you do

5. The organisation as a whole

6. The 'cause' or common purpose.

When all of those potentially different directions are aligned, it's far easier to commit. When any one diverges from the others, then like anyone else you'll experience a degree of tension. We'll return to that divergence in Lesson 9, when we focus on the role of courage and the ways it complements commitment (to your boss and others) but can also sometimes be at odds with it.

For now, to help you answer that question "Commitment to what?" I'll paraphrase Ira Chaleff, who points out that a leader and their people "both orbit around the purpose"; the leader's staff do not orbit around the leader[81]. As you progress through this lesson, I'd ask that you bear that phrase in mind whenever you find yourself wondering what it is you're meant to be committing to.

Managing your own commitment

Your success and your impact on your boss will largely be determined by your ability to keep going and your preparedness to go beyond your official remit, in the face of numerous obstacles and temptations to take the easier route.

On those occasions when your commitment wanes, it's important to ask why. The easy answer will be to blame external factors – your boss, your customers or clients, your workload, the culture, size or bureaucracy of the organisation, and so on. More productive, typically, is to turn that question inwardly as well as outwardly, asking "What is it in me that needs to change to renew my commitment?" as well as "What could I change in my environment to ensure I am (and stay) genuinely engaged?"

Understanding your commitment

Where the Three Core Disciplines and the ARC Qualities are concerned, we already know that the commitment of the people around us will have an impact on our own commitment. Having a clear *direction* makes a huge difference, too, whether that's the direction we've chosen for ourselves and our career (which you can explore in Lesson 1 if you've not already done so) or the direction we've agreed and clarified with our bosses (which is the focus of Lesson 5). A direction that feels *authentic* – i.e. one that's aligned with our values and feels like "a prize worth fighting for"[82] – will fuel our commitment. If

the direction we're heading feels inauthentic, it'll be sapping our energy. Similarly, if that direction is consistent with our existing *responsibilities* – to others and to ourselves, both on the work and personal fronts – then it'll require less additional effort to stay committed. If it's at odds with our other responsibilities – if it conflicts with other needs we have – then that tension will always be chipping away at our commitment.

Responsibility has another part to play, too. It's a word that's often associated with accountability, and accountability is a key ingredient for commitment. If I'm not held to account then sadly I'm less likely to deliver. If I feel others around me are being let off the hook, then I'm also less likely to take accountability – and thus my commitments – seriously. This is true even when we set goals for ourselves.

Looking at *direction* in the shorter term, the basic psychology of motivation tells us it's also easier to stay committed when we set clear, tangible targets or milestones and reward ourselves for achieving them. So it's worth taking a few moments to decide what reward you'll give yourself as you tick off each of the things you want to achieve.

Capacity will also serve to enable or inhibit commitment. It's hard to stay motivated if you've a constant nagging feeling that you don't have the necessary skills, knowledge or resources to get the job done, or if the processes around you feel like obstacles, or the structure in which you're working seems to be limiting your ability to perform.

What role does *courage* play? We'll look at that closer in Lesson 9. For now, it's enough to recognise three things. Firstly, that it sometimes takes courage to stay committed in the face of significant challenges. Secondly, that productive conflict is a key ingredient in securing commitment. After all, if I feel I can't air my concerns that the objective or the proposed approach to achieving it are flawed, then those concerns will make it very hard for me to commit – perhaps rightly so. Thirdly, it takes courage to engage in that productive conflict.

Finally, we've already touched on the role of other people's commitment in influencing our own, but another important ingredient where commitment is concerned is trust: do I trust the people whose commitment is required for me to succeed in fulfilling this objective? If I don't feel they're being authentic, or if I feel unable to be authentic with them – sharing what I see, think and feel – then trust will be hard to come by.

To examine your own commitment to a current objective, and what feeds and starves it, start by articulating that objective in the space below. It should be something significant and reasonably long term.

Now, in the following diagram, rate (from 0 – 10) the extent to which each of the statements is true in relation to your stated objective. In case you'd rather not write in this book, you'll also find a copy on the *Boss Factor* resources page at www.leaderspace.com.

The direction is clear

I have clear and meaningful milestones along the way

The objective is aligned with my values

The objective feels 'worth fighting for'

The objective is aligned with my other needs and responsibilities

I feel accountable for its success

I feel I have sufficient authority to live up to that accountability

I trust the people around me whose support is critical to my success

I have their full commitment

I have (or have access to) the required knowledge and skills

I have the necessary resources to do the job

I feel able to speak up about any doubts I have regarding the objective and/or the proposed ways of achieving it

I feel able to hold others to account for their part in delivering on the objective

DIRECTION

AUTHENTIC

RESPONSIBLE

SELF
TEAM
ORGANISATION

COMMITMENT

CAPACITY

COURAGEOUS

Increasing your commitment

When you look at the ratings above, what do they suggest you can do to further enhance your commitment?

....

....

....

....

....

....

....

....

If your commitment is suffering and it feels like a lack of capacity is a contributing factor, you'll likely benefit from spending some time on Lesson 7 ('Continually build your capacity') if you haven't already – if you have, you might want to revisit it with this particular objective in mind. If you scored lower on the statements related to courage, you should find Lesson 9 ('Be courageous') particularly helpful. If the objective doesn't feel authentic or meaningful enough for you, then you might need to do more with Lessons 1 ('Have a vision of your own') and/or 2 ('Choose your leader wisely'). If trust is an issue, it's worth applying the levers of trust outlined in Lesson 6 ('Take due responsibility'). If you feel you're lacking the full commitment of key stakeholders, you'll find help in the second half of this current lesson.

Drains and energisers

Sometimes the easiest route to managing our commitment is to identify the things that most energise us and the things that most drain that energy.

Take a moment to write down the names of the five people or things (at work and outside of work) that most energise you when it comes to achieving the objective you outlined above:

....

....

....

Now write down the names of up to five people or things that might drain your enthusiasm for that goal (for example, by talking negatively about the goal or actively blocking your progress):

....

....

....

When you look at those lists, what do you realise you could be doing differently? It's easy to assume you should simply avoid the second group and spend more time engaging with the first. However, some of the people in the second group might need you to win them over, which we'll look at later in this lesson. Others may be being inadvertently helpful: there may be ways you can turn their doubts or resistance into fuel for yourself. For instance, one of my clients had a senior stakeholder tell him he had no solid business case for something he was proposing. It felt like a real knock-back at the time, but subsequently inspired my client to invest time in creating something far more robust and compelling.

Breathing, sleeping well and eating frogs for breakfast

The most immediate impact of capacity on commitment, though, comes when our physiological capacity is depleted. It takes physical energy to get things done, to maintain morale and determination – particularly under pressure. So it's no surprise that our commitment typically wanes when we're not drinking, eating and sleeping healthily, or getting enough fresh air and exercise. Too many of the people I've worked with have lost touch with the fact that their brains are fed by their bodies and won't function properly if their bodies are a mess.

While we're on the subject of eating healthily, our commitment can benefit from instilling a discipline of "eating the frog"[83]. This isn't a popular expression in our house, as my daughter's first pet was a frog, but – as you're probably hoping – it's a metaphor, not a food supplement! The frog in question is whatever we're procrastinating over at a given moment – perhaps a difficult email or call, or a dull and bulky report in need of review. Brian Tracy, who popularised the term, suggests starting with the frog as the first thing of the day. That way, everything that follows will be a relative joy, and when our day feels like it's getting better it's bound to boost our commitment.

Finally, it takes literal, physical energy to pretend we're someone or something we're not. It's also fairly unrewarding to get to the end of each day knowing we're faking it. So anything you can do to ensure you're feeling authentic in the work you're doing will boost your commitment.

You'll find further tips on maintaining commitment in books by Roy Baumeister and Kelly McGonigal[84]. Personally, if you're as time-poor as most people, I'd recommend choosing just one book as there's a fair bit of overlap between them

Securing and maintaining the commitment of others

Commitment to what?

Before we look at whose commitment we want to secure and maintain, and how to do so, you'll need to decide what you want the focus of that commitment to be. We looked at this already on page 177. I'd encourage you to focus on people's commitment to the shared endeavour, that higher purpose for which you and your boss are responsible.

You might choose something else, though. You might even choose to focus the rest of your efforts in this lesson on people's commitment to you. If you do, you'll have missed one of the core messages of this book, but I'll understand. There's got to be something in it for you, after all. I'd ask, though, that you focus on the shared endeavour, too – either first, or after you've focused on yourself. After all, if you can align the two, you'll have everyone aligned around something that benefits you and the wider organisation.

Whose commitment?

Given the focus of this book, we'll obviously want to include your boss's commitment. Too few people attend to the waxing and waning of their boss's commitment over time, other than to complain about it. The most mature recognise that the 'boss' seat is a lonely one that is almost always occupied by human beings who have their own ups and downs in life. These people recognise that one of the key causes of waning commitment in leaders is the challenge of balancing the complex and competing needs of their own bosses and those of the people they lead.

Statistically speaking, there's a significant probability that at least some of the other people working for your boss are less than 100% engaged. These people will be making life harder for your boss and they'll be making life harder for you. The easy – some would say "lazy" – approach is to write these people off, to blame them for their apparent lack of commitment. An easy alternative is to blame the boss or more distant factors like culture, organisational performance or difficult customers. As we'll see, there are more helpful, proactive and enabling ways to approach such a situation. Given that a key role for our bosses is managing the commitment of the people they lead, anything we can do to facilitate that will be adding value. Unbridled optimism and constant cheerleading for our bosses smacks of sycophancy and will rarely go down well, but positivity will work in moderation.

Finally, there's the commitment of the other stakeholders on whom your success and your boss's success depend. These are the people who'll make or break the shared endeavour from the outside. They're the people who hold the purse strings, the political strings, the critical resources, the vetoes, the power to be enablers or bottlenecks. They're the people whose commitment – or lack of it – will keep your boss awake at night. They're the people at your boss's level and above whose opinions of you could shape your future career.

If you're keen to explore commitment amongst your various stakeholders, including your boss and peers, it's worth skipping ahead briefly to the table on page 196 and filling out the first two columns, then coming back here. In that table you'll name some key stakeholders and rate their current levels of commitment. The table is there, not here, because you'll use it to record any ideas and actions in the third column towards the end of this lesson. Between now and then we'll be exploring the various factors that'll be affecting those people's commitment and the things you can do to increase the commitment of anyone.

Understanding their commitment

To influence our bosses or stakeholders, we need to understand them. To do so, I've found it helpful to ask the following five key questions, each tapping into different statements in an assessment of their commitment:

1. What do they need? Which of those needs are being met and not met?

Most people say they don't like engaging in workplace politics and they dislike and disparage those who do. Indeed, to many, 'office politics' is virtually a swearword. It's true that some 'office politicians' are manipulative and we don't need people like that in the workplace. What we do need, though, is people who understand people, people who understand what's come to be called 'The Boston-Miah paradigm': that what many people call 'politics' is actually "the appreciation and management of stakeholders' explicit *and implicit* needs."[85] Seen in that light, it's just common sense. If what you or I are proposing meets people's needs, then they're more likely to commit. If our proposals prevent or distract them from getting their needs met, then they'll struggle to commit and – arguably – they'd be stupid to do so.

Some needs are spoken aloud, some are obvious, some are easy to guess at and some are buried deep. For the first two, it's worth working up a list for each person. For the latter two, it can help to think in terms of those three fundamental human needs proposed by Will Schutz that we first encountered in Lesson 4[86]. To recap, all of us need these three things, but we need them in different amounts. If we get too much or too little, we're left feeling uncomfortable, dissatisfied, frustrated or even distressed.

- *Inclusion / involvement / significance:* we all need to feel significant and dislike being excluded from the conversations, decisions, communications, meetings and relationships that are important to us. At the same time, most of us have a threshold for inclusion and dislike being dragged into things we don't consider sufficiently important.

- *Control / influence / recognition:* we vary in the extent to which we want to control others and be controlled by them. We each need a certain amount of power and responsibility (no more and no less) and to feel competent in the work we do. Even if your boss says all they want is results, it's most likely because of their need to feel a sense of control and to feel reassured that they're doing a competent job as your leader.

- *Affection / connection / appreciation:* we might not all want to be loved by everyone, but all of us want to be loved by someone. In the workplace, it's usually about being liked, rather than loved. It's about being appreciated for who we are and what we bring as individuals.

At work, people often belittle the last of those three, but it's a key driver when it comes to trust and it's the 'magic' that lies at the heart of most successful relationships and teams. Importantly, our need to be liked is also tied to our need for openness, i.e. to share personal information and have others share it with us.

It's worth considering the extent to which your boss, peers and other stakeholders are getting these and their other needs met. If you and the things you're looking to achieve are helping *them* meet *their* needs, then you're an ally and you'll be more likely to secure and maintain their commitment – particularly if they've few other people helping them meet those needs. If you're not helping, you're likely to be somewhat irrelevant. If you're getting in the way, then you're going to have a really hard time gaining their buy-in.

2. What lies in their past and probable future?

The more we know about someone's past, the more we know about their present. Our patterns of thinking and behaving are formed by experience. The experiences that influence us most are those we had in childhood and our early working lives. However, the events of an individual's past few hours, months or years will tell you a lot about how they're feeling right now. Were they made redundant two years ago? Were they on holiday last week? Did they have a particularly difficult meeting right before they met with you? All of these things will influence the extent to which they'll give you, your boss or your team their full commitment.

Similarly, it's helpful to ask ourselves what lies in this person's future. Their age might give us some generic clues to what the next five years has in store for them: the desire for promotion or retirement, marriage, kids, empty nest, dying friends, frail parents, first home, and so on. We might also have information on upcoming events in their work calendar or changes to their role or the structure of their department. All of these factors will affect their needs and mind-set; each could be a help or a hindrance to you gaining their buy-in to a proposal or course of action. So you might start by exploring what else they've got on today, then factoring that into your approach to securing their commitment.

3. Who else might be boosting or draining their commitment?

Most of us live at the centre of our own universe. It's difficult to see the world consistently from any other perspective. So if you place yourself in your boss's (or other stakeholder's) shoes and look at who is above, below and around them, who do you see? Who's vying for their attention? Who do they trust and not trust? Whose needs are they trying to meet, juggle and/or prioritise? Who are their friends, their allies, their minions, their enablers, their obstacles, their customers, etc.? Who are the drains and energisers around them? What's going on for them outside of work that could be distracting them or making it harder for them to commit?

4. What beliefs, assumptions and expectations are affecting their commitment?

If you've delved into Lesson 3, you'll already have a fairly deep insight into your mind-set regarding your relationship with your boss, your boss's role and the nature of the world around you. You'll probably also have insights into your boss's mind-set – their ways of viewing the world, the beliefs, assumptions and expectations they hold. If you've already managed to put yourself in your boss's shoes over the past couple of pages, then you'll be in a good position to answer the following questions about their mind-set. I'd encourage you to apply these questions to the other stakeholder you're considering, too.

- What are their assumptions about themselves and the world?

- Relative to others, are they more optimistic or more pessimistic?

- Do they currently feel 'in control' of their own destiny or caught in the currents around them?

- When it comes to relationships, do they tend towards compliance, defiance, self-reliance, compromise or collaborative interdependence?

- What are their expectations of you and the people around them?

5. How do they prefer to communicate and make decisions?

It's generally easier to secure and maintain people's commitment if we speak in their language. That's why tools that help us understand how different people prefer to communicate and make decisions are so helpful. They prompt us to ask questions like:[87]

- Do they prefer written or verbal communication?

- Do they want detail or just the headlines?

- Do they want hard evidence or bold, innovative speculation?

- Do they value 'small talk' or prefer to get straight down to business?

- Do they want the agenda and/or preparatory information in advance, or would they be more energised by an emergent, evolving conversation?

- Do they expect quick, clear, final decisions with full commitment or do they need to know there's scope for further discussion and/or withdrawal if they have second thoughts?

Increasing their commitment

Once we've understood people's current commitment and the reasons for it, we're in a far better position to increase that commitment should we need to. We'll take a few minutes now to assess the current commitment of your boss and the other key stakeholder you've had in mind throughout this lesson. From that will emerge some ideas as to how to enhance their commitment, should it need enhancing.

Focusing on your boss

As mentioned earlier, I recommend using the diagram below to clarify your understanding of your boss's current commitment, by rating (from 0 – 10) the extent to which each of the statements is true in relation to their current objective(s). Again, you'll find a copy at www.leaderspace.com.

My boss's objective/objectives is/are clear to them

My boss has clear and meaningful milestones along the way

The objective is aligned with my boss's values and fits with their current ways of viewing the world

My boss's objective/objectives is/are aligned with their other needs and responsibilities

The objective feels 'worth fighting for' to them

They feel accountable

They feel they have sufficient authority to live up to that accountability

They trust the people around them whose support is critical to their success

They believe they have (or have access to) the required knowledge and skills

They believe the key people on whom this objective relies are fully committed themselves

They believe they have the necessary resources to do the job

They feel able to challenge the people in power around them

They feel able to hold people to account for their part in delivering on the objective

DIRECTION
AUTHENTIC
RESPONSIBLE
SELF TEAM ORGANISATION
COMMITMENT
CAPACITY
COURAGEOUS

When you look at the ratings above, what do they suggest you can do to further enhance your boss's commitment?

....

....

....

If you're looking for inspiration to answer the question above, you might find it helpful to consider the following:

- If their commitment is low and it seems a lack of clarity is a contributing factor, Lesson 5 ('Seek clarity') could help as the basis for a conversation with them

- If lack of capacity is undermining their commitment, it's worth considering what additional responsibilities you can take on (Lesson 6) and/or how you can create additional capacity in the system around you (Lesson 7)

- If their objectives seem out of kilter with their values, their ways of viewing the world, or other needs and responsibilities, they might benefit from Lessons 1, 3, 4 or 6 respectively. They might even take a look at their relationship with their own boss, perhaps starting with Lesson 2 ('Choose your leader wisely')

- If they're struggling with trust, they might benefit from doing some work with you on the levers of trust outlined on page 147

- If courage and/or holding people to account are proving difficult, then it's worth turning to Lesson 9 ('Be courageous') for inspiration

- If they're feeling they lack the commitment of their key stakeholders, then you could help them by drawing on the influencing tips later in this current lesson.

Focusing on other stakeholders

Now turn your attention to another key stakeholder. Again, rate (from 0 – 10) the extent to which each of the statements is true in relation to whatever objective is of greatest interest to you. For instance, a 'shared endeavour' for which you and/or your boss need their buy in.

The objective is clear

The objective and means of achieving it are aligned with the overall objectives of the organisation

The objective and ways of achieving it are aligned with their values and fit with their current ways of viewing the world

The objective feels 'worth fighting for' to them

They trust you and everyone else involved

They believe the key people on whom this objective relies are fully committed themselves

The objective is aligned with their other needs and responsibilities

They feel accountable for their part in making this a success

They believe you have (or have access to) the necessary knowledge, skills and resources to fulfil the objective

They feel they've capacity to provide any additional support required

The decision-making and communication processes suit their needs and preferences

They feel able to air any doubts they have regarding the objective and/or the proposed ways of achieving it

They believe the people involved will be held to account for making this a success

193

When you look at the ratings above, what do they suggest you can do to further enhance this person's commitment?

....

....

....

....

As with your boss, you'll find some keys to enhancing this stakeholder's commitment in some of the other lessons in this book. If you're still struggling to get them on board, then I'd recommend deploying some of the following techniques to secure their buy-in.

The art of influence

Remember the tale of the Pied Piper of Hamlin, who was able to charm rats and children alike with a compelling tune? Influencing works much the same way. There are a number of different notes to choose from and it's the combination of notes that gets us moving. It might well be that there's one 'perfect tune' that'll secure commitment from everyone, just like the Pied Piper's, but until we find it, it's likely to be a case of finding the right tune for your intended audience.

I've found the following twelve[88] 'notes' helpful when discussing influencing with clients. Most of us play just one or two, maybe three. Few use all twelve and, personally, I find one or two rather distasteful, but they all work and I'd encourage you to think about which of the twelve you use most and which you might experiment with to further enhance your ability to secure and maintain commitment.

- Use facts, figures and logic – you'll need to be able to back them up, even in a 'post truth' world, and you'll need to bear in mind your audience's tolerance for detail

- Paint a compelling, inspiring vision of the future – or a terrifying vision of what might happen if you're unable to achieve what you're looking to achieve

- Offer them something in return – ideally something that'll cost you less than you'll gain from their commitment to you

- Take it to the brink – show them you're willing to risk mutually-assured destruction if they don't give you their full commitment

- Ask for their support as a personal favour – but beware of the risk that the favour they'll ask in return will cost more than you gained from their support

- Give something for free – supermarkets have been doing this for years to build customer loyalty

- Ask questions – develop your understanding of their needs, concerns and potential reasons to resist or buy into your proposals

- Draw on allies – whether that's by referencing the people who are already on board or asking those allies to advocate on your behalf

- Use 'physical intimidation' – I don't mean threats, violence or abuse (which are immoral and generally illegal), but you'll have noticed yourself that people who seem physically bigger and stronger than us (or invade our personal space) often leave us feeling we ought to comply

- Flatter them – sycophancy is pretty transparent, but people are more amenable when they're in a good mood, so it doesn't hurt to drop some genuine compliments

- Deploy drugs and alcohol – people have been using legal drugs like caffeine, nicotine, sugar and booze to 'sweeten the deal' for centuries, despite the fact that virtually all of us can easily spot a schmooze

- Play the 'formal authority' card – this is very much a last resort as it tends to breed compliance rather than commitment, but if it's all you have left to you then it is a valid 'note' to play. There's also the option of using 'borrowed authority', meaning telling people (truthfully) that someone more senior than you want this thing done.

If you've identified the notes you play and the notes you don't, you'll likely have some ideas for new approaches to securing commitment from your boss, peers and other stakeholders.

From ideas to actions

We've covered a lot of ground in this lesson and it's time to pull all that thinking together. On page 186 I suggested you complete the first two columns in the following table. Whether you did it then or not, I'd encourage you to use it to assess the current commitment of your boss, peers and other stakeholders and then to record the ideas you have for increasing their commitment, and the actions you're going to take as a result.

Stakeholder's name (including boss and peers)	Current commitment (0-10)	Ideas and actions

Stakeholder's name (including boss and peers)	Current commitment (0-10)	Ideas and actions

Applying this lesson as a leader of others

If you're a leader in your own right, you're probably already thinking about the role of commitment in your relationships with the people you lead – perhaps even the impact it has on your commitment when their commitment waxes and wanes. Most leaders have a reasonable handle on which of their people are most and least committed. Some notice the waxing and waning of people's commitment, and the role the leader plays in that ebb and flow. Others write people off as either committed or not, and pay little attention to the part they play.

How much do you understand the reasons why commitment varies across the people you lead? What feeds and starves their commitment? What is it they're committed (or not committed) to? Is it you? Is it the organisation? The team? The shared endeavour? You can use any of the tools from this lesson to help deepen your understanding of your people's commitment and as food for discussion – either one-to-one or as a team. You might also be thinking about adding some extra 'notes' to the tune you use to influence the people you lead, enhancing your ability to secure their commitment.

You might be wondering, too, about the influence of your stakeholders' commitment on the commitment of the people you lead – and vice versa. You might be curious about the possibility of giving your people greater responsibility for getting stakeholders on board, particularly if you tend to take on all of that responsibility yourself, or if there's someone in the team who might be better at it than you, or someone who'd benefit from the development offered by having greater exposure to important stakeholders – and the opportunity to expand *their* repertoire of 'notes' when it comes to influencing others.

In summary

Without a clear direction, we'll go nowhere; without the necessary capacity we'll struggle to make it to our destination; without sufficient commitment we might never even get started. We'll certainly find it hard to keep going when in the face of setbacks, obstacles and nasty surprises. So we've focused on your commitment, your boss's commitment and the commitment of the people you both rely on to get things done.

We asked what it is you (and they) are committed to. We deepened your understanding of the forces behind the waxing and waning of commitment. We looked at ways of managing your own commitment and others', including twelve influencing styles. If you've answered the questions posed, you'll have assessed a number of stakeholders' current levels of commitment, done a deeper dive with your boss and you'll have some clear actions to take to boost any commitment that's lagging or lacking.

• ● •

Lesson 9:
Be courageous

- How courage is key to delivering on each of the lessons in this book

- What do we mean by 'courage' in the workplace?

- What happens when courage and commitment collide?

- How to boost your courage – both temporarily and for the longer term

COURAGE HAS BEEN A THREAD throughout this book and

in this lesson I'll define courage in a work context and summarise the three types of courageous action that are most relevant to your relationship with your boss. Then we'll look at the interaction between courage and commitment, which is important in a range of contexts but probably more so in this particular relationship. Then I'll share some practical tips for boosting your courage if and when you need it.

One caveat: 'courageous' is the 'C' in *ARC Leadership*[89], so – as in Lesson 6 when we looked at responsibility (the 'R') – I'll be doing my best to build on the content of my previous book while providing a lesson that stands on its own. I've had to be very, very focused here so, if you do want to take a deeper dive, you know where to look.

A crash course in courage

I reckon the best definition comes from the late Susan Jeffers: "feel the fear and do it anyway"[90]. In my own research, I found three 'dimensions' to courage: the nature of the fear you're facing, the kind of courageous action you're taking when you're "doing it anyway" and the amount of time you do it for – there's a big difference between being courageous for a few minutes in a meeting and persevering in the face of adversity for weeks, months or years.

> "Instead of viewing followers as the 'good soldiers' who carry out commands dutifully, we need to view followers as the primary defenders against toxic leaders or dysfunctional organizations"
>
> Robert E. Kelley,[91]
> Consultant and business school professor at Carnegie Mellon University

For our purposes, it's enough to focus here on the three types of courageous action that are most relevant to your relationship with your boss: moral, intellectual and aspirational.

We show **moral courage** when we challenge something we believe is illegal or ethically wrong or choose a path we believe is ethically right knowing that path will be hard to tread. For instance, if your boss is sanctioning cheating on emissions tests (like at Volkswagen), cutting costs at the expense of safety (as happened at BP), condoning irresponsible or illegal banking practices, bullying you or other employees, or failing to hold people sufficiently to account. Moral courage can equally be about standing *beside* your boss to help them do the right thing, which includes backing them when they take a stand and supporting a leader who's trying to change their own disruptive, dysfunctional or less-than-optimal ways of working. Finally, as we'll see below, it can be moral courage that causes us to leave a boss, team or organisation.

Intellectual courage is one of the most common qualities the leaders I speak to seek in the people they lead. We show intellectual courage when we challenge the status quo; when we question our own or others' decisions, assertions, opinions or assumptions on the grounds that they're illogical, factually incorrect, unverifiable or out of date; when we take a truly novel or creative approach to a situation or propose a new way of doing things that might meet with resistance, confusion or ridicule. It's intellectual courage that was lacking in a senior manager I knew in a well-known manufacturing company, when he knew that providing resources to bolster a colleague's failing department was crippling his own multimillion dollar project but he soldiered on without pushing back or asking for help or an extension, causing him to blow his budget and finish well behind time.

We show **aspirational courage** when we strive against adversity to achieve something truly ambitious; when we take a bold idea or vision and work hard to make it a reality; when we simply strive to be better today than we were yesterday. Your levels of aspirational courage will have influenced how you approached Lesson 1 ('Have a vision'), for instance, and Lesson 7 ('Continually build your capacity').

As I mentioned when outlining moral courage, it often takes courage to leave a boss, team or organisation – particularly if that comes at significant

Courageous responsibility with a bullying boss

Helping a leader change their own destructive but deep-rooted habits can require us to change the way *we* operate if our old behaviours were somehow reinforcing theirs. For instance, if we've been responding to (what feels like) bullying by scurrying off and doing as we're told, then we'll have been rewarding and thus encouraging them to bully us. As Pavlov's dogs taught us, the easiest way to change a behaviour is to change the response it gets. So, to break the pattern, we and the rest of their people will need to stand up to that behaviour each and every time it occurs.

financial, reputational, practical and/or emotional cost. The nature of that courage will depend on the reasons for leaving. Perhaps you believe you've done all the growing you can do, or the team or its leader can't grow any further while you remain. Perhaps you've run out of commitment and – though you've tried – you can't find a way to renew it. Perhaps, despite your best efforts, you've been unable to prevent unethical or abhorrent behaviour or help your boss fill a gap in their competence. Perhaps you've found yourself incapable of or prevented from providing or securing the skills or resources the team or organisation needs to keep moving forward. As long as you've already done everything you can to rectify the situation, each of these is an example of doing the right thing despite pressures or temptations to do otherwise[92].

Thinking about your current work situation and relationship with your boss, to what extent are you currently demonstrating each of these three types of courage (moral, intellectual, aspirational)?

Which of the three is most needed if you're to take your work and/or this relationship to the next level?

When courage meets commitment

"Dan's cruising to the end of his career and doesn't seem to have any interest in getting out of his comfort zone," said a senior leader, Jules, of one of her staff. "He's basically a blocker, not an enabler, when it comes to our vision as a department."

What Jules was seeing was a lack of aspirational courage and a lack of true commitment to that overarching vision. At the time, she didn't know what was causing the problem. A general lack of courage could have been making it harder for Dan to commit to the vision, for fear of what it entailed. Doubts about the vision itself could have been the issue, increasing the fear and reducing the willingness to 'do it anyway'. Perhaps both causes were in play, with courage and commitment playing off of each other in a vicious circle. Perhaps there was an entirely separate common cause – something at work or outside of work; something current or something entirely rooted in Dan's past.

The important thing for us, here and now, is that Jules hadn't really thought beyond the behaviour she was seeing. She didn't have time and Dan hadn't made it easy for her. So she'd put Dan in a box and she was probably going to either leave him there or get rid of him. The box in question would have been the bottom left in the following 2 x 2 grid[93].

People in the bottom left I've chosen to call 'Passive resistors'. Like Dan, they'll be seen by their bosses as blockers, not enablers. Like Dan, they'll have their reasons for feeling unable to commit to the shared endeavour. However, for some reason, they're not courageous enough to push back: their resistance is passive not active. You can tell if you're one of these people if you complain to others about your boss, the direction in which they're taking you or the work you're doing, but never address these issues directly with them. You're a passive resistor if you cut corners, put in minimal effort, take unnecessary time off or resist going beyond your official remit when your boss, task, team or stakeholders need it.

You're a 'rebel' if you're unwilling or unable to commit and you're prepared to speak up. You'll see yourself as something of a hero, and other rebels and passive resistors will agree with you. You might be right: the challenge you bring could be exactly what's needed if current ways of working are ineffective, dysfunctional or destructive. You might be wrong: rebels can destabilise a team and potentially the wider system, wrecking relationships, weakening the leader and spreading discord amongst team members and key stakeholders. Whether, as a rebel, you're a hero or a villain isn't simply a matter of perspective. It'll be determined in part by the relationship mind-set you bring to the situation and the extent to which that mind-set is appropriate to the situation or simply a pattern you're prone to repeating wherever you go. So, if you're currently in 'rebel' mode, then if you haven't already done so I'd recommend investing in Lesson 3 ('Challenge your assumptions').

Whether you find it there or elsewhere, it'll be easier to create change if you can find some common ground to which you and your apparent adversaries *can* jointly commit. You'll find it easier to build trust between you and easier to explore the reasons you're finding it hard to commit.

Moving to the opposite corner of our 2 x 2 grid we find the 'devotees' who are fully committed. "Committed to what?" you might ask*. "The boss? The team? The organisation? The cause we're 'fighting' for?"

You'd be right to ask. When we're looking at the grid above, you could arguably put whatever commitment you like along the vertical axis. Your choice will likely affect where you place yourself (and others) in the grid, but it could also have some pretty serious ramifications for you, your boss, the relationship between you and the way you view your peers.

Label the vertical axis 'Commitment to the boss' and we risk making the same mistake I believe one of the leading writers on followership, Robert E. Kelley[94], made when he labelled people in this place on our grid 'Yes Men' and people a little further down that commitment axis 'Sheep'. These terms seem unnecessarily derogatory to me**, doing a disservice to the contributions you and others can make by being fully committed (assuming you've the necessary capacity to do the job), even if you're not currently particularly courageous. These, after all, are people displaying a great deal of loyalty – something every leader's looking for in the people they lead[95], which is why so many of the executives attending Kelley's seminars said they'd prefer most of their people to be in the top left of our grid.

---

* We addressed this question early in Lesson 8, when we looked directly at your ability to secure and maintain your own and others' commitment.

** The words 'Yes Men' and 'Sheep' also suggest the person's current behaviours are the result of defining, fixed or in-built traits, whereas there'll be a number of factors influencing the extent to which any member of staff displays commitment and courage at work.

Loyalty is a great quality... except when it's not. Sometimes we need to prioritise commitment to a 'higher cause' over commitment to an individual, heeding Ira Chaleff's call for leaders and their people to "orbit the purpose", rather than the followers orbiting the leader[96]. If we don't, we risk following the path of those 'devotees' at Merck whose appalling, life-threatening manipulation of drug trial data scost the pharmaceuticals giant over US$5 billion – twice the profit the company made from the medication in question[97].

Whether the commitment you choose to put on the vertical axis of our 2 x 2 grid is commitment to your boss, your team, your organisation or a higher purpose, if you're fully committed and highly courageous you're likely to thrive. Being in that top right position on the grid with the other 'trail-blazers' means you're just as keen as the devotees to go the extra mile to make the boss, team or organisation successful, or to deliver on that higher cause. However, you also believe that being morally, intellectually and aspirationally courageous will achieve far more than commitment alone. As Kelley observes, you'll offer your boss constructive feedback, you'll have earned their trust and – if you want it – you'll have a place at their right hand as a leader amongst your peers.

Importantly, I prefer the term 'trail-blazers' to Kelley's term 'stars', for two reasons. Firstly, because you might not be a star if you're only delivering on Lessons 8 and 9 of the ten in this book, which is all that the grid in this lesson addresses. Secondly, because Kelley found that it's rare for an executive to want a team entirely comprised of people who are both highly committed and highly courageous. I can understand that, but I find it harder to imagine your boss saying they wouldn't want a team full of 'stars' than to imagine them admitting their concerns about a team full of trail-blazers. For instance, if you're a trail-blazer your boss might worry that you'll grow bored, disillusioned or difficult to manage.

Like Kelley, I believe the true stars are those who don't just demand or wait passively for stimulation: they become self-sustaining. So, with a team full of fantastic followers, your boss's only real concern should be how to develop him or herself enough that they can step up to give you and your peers sufficient space to flourish.

Trail-blazers in the field

Trail-blazers include the classic grizzled regimental sergeant major who role-models respect for his less-experienced commanding officer (CO) when interacting with his peers and subordinates, and privately offers supportive challenge to his CO in the spirit of providing the full benefit of his years on the battlefield. We see similar behaviours in England's World Cup winning rugby team of 2003[98], where captain Martin Johnson was supported by some great 'sub leaders' on the field: great followers who would challenge him quietly so as not to undermine his authority. Subsequent, less effective and less celebrated teams have arguably lacked that calibre and culture of followership.

Trail-blazers are courageous in their relationship with their boss, their peers, the people above and below them, and with their other stakeholders. They're also courageous in the way they think about and treat themselves – which you've been encouraged to do consistently throughout this book.

In a moment, we'll look at ways to boost your courage if and when it needs that boost. Before we do, take a moment to extract maximum value from the last few pages by answering the following questions.

In your current team, or in each of the teams you are part of, where are you now on the 'courage vs commitment' grid? *(Decide in advance what it is you're measuring your commitment to, then mark yourself on the grid below).*

COMMITMENT

COURAGE

What has brought you to that point in the grid, and what's keeping you there? *(Challenge yourself to consider the factors within you as well as the things your boss has done and other external factors.)*

....

....

....

If you were given a sudden but lasting boost in courage, what would you do differently?

....

....

....

Boosting your courage if and when you need it

There are lots[99] of forces working within you when it comes to being courageous at work, including your natural survival instincts and the pressure to be responsible and loyal to the people around you, which it's easy to interpret as meaning toeing the line and doing what you're told. There are cultural factors, too: challenging or standing up to your boss is generally more acceptable in current American and British cultures than it has traditionally been in Chinese or Japanese cultures, for example.

With all those forces to contend with, I recommend being both strategic and tactical when it comes to developing your courage. The strategies below focus on strengthening your underlying courage 'muscle' – which really *is* a thing! The tactics are a collection of tips aimed at helping you muster courage in the moment.

Strategies: strengthening your courage 'muscle'

1. Change your mind-set, shift your identity

Our beliefs and assumptions about ourselves and the world around us – our mind-sets – have a massive influence on our behaviour. Most of us suffer from "courage blindness"[100], a term coined by "the Indiana Jones of Psychology", Robert Biswas-Diener, to refer to our tendency to assume courage is something displayed only by celebrated, medal-winning heroes, not in the everyday lives of ordinary people. Add to this a dose of 'impostor syndrome'[101], which seems to afflict the majority of people I've met, and you've the ingredients for a mind-set that'll have you convinced that being courageous in your relationship with your boss is either beyond you or really, really hard. When that mind-set causes you to describe yourself as "not a courageous person", you've made a lack of courage part of your identity. It isn't. It's just a belief and you've changed hundreds of beliefs in the course of your life. This is just another.

One way of shifting those beliefs by yourself is to look for the evidence that you're actually a lot more courageous than you give yourself credit for. So, if you're keen to give it a go, start by writing down at least five things you've done in your life that required you to "feel the fear and do it anyway"*. It doesn't matter what they are or in what context these things happened. It's just important that you recognise them and that there was some kind of fear involved.

....

....

....

---

* "Feel the Fear and Do It Anyway" is a registered trademark of The Jeffers / Shelmerdine Family Trust, used with their permission

....

....

....

....

....

....

2. Notice what you're practising[102]

Every time we repeat a behaviour we're practising it. The more we practice it, the more habitual, automated and fixed that behaviour becomes. This is as true of unhelpful behaviours as it is of helpful ones. Thus, if I sit quietly in a meeting when I know the right thing to do is to speak up, then I'm practising keeping quiet when I know the right thing to do is to speak up.

To adapt a lesson from Susan Scott, author of *Fierce Leadership*[103], think of a current or recent situation in which you'd like to be, or to *have been*, more courageous. Then complete the following sentences.

In approaching this situation the way I'm approaching it, I'm practising...

....

....

....

....

....

I could be practising being more courageous in relation to this situation by...

....

....

....

....

....

....

3. Release the pressure

The first two strategies focused on helping you "feel the fear" but "do it anyway". You can also work on reducing the fear. At a strategic level, you'll get a significant pay-off if you invest time in meditation, mindfulness or taking a relaxing walk every day. Tactically, you'll be amazed how effective it can be to simply notice where the tension is in your body when you feel the fear rising and threatening to overwhelm your courage. Once you've located that fear in a particular muscle or muscle group, focus on relaxing that muscle or muscles and you'll feel the fear subside. The more you do it, the more effective it'll be.

Tactics: mustering courage in the moment

Courage in your relationship with your boss can take many forms. You might be considering an act of moral courage against unethical or inappropriate behaviour. It could be an act of intellectual courage challenging the status quo, limited perspectives or faulty thinking. Maybe you're keen to show aspirational courage by calling on your leader to be bigger and bolder in their ambitions for the team or organisation. You might believe your boss's agenda has diverged from that of the team, the wider organisation, its core purpose, its stakeholders and/or the core tenets you agreed when you first started working together.

Perhaps you've become convinced that your boss has been promoted into a role that's outside their areas of competence, is struggling to keep up or handle increasing complexity – either because they lack the skills or intellect, or because they're exhausted or ill, or overwhelmed by other pressures inside or outside of work. It could even be that you've decided it's the right thing for you to leave your boss but are concerned about the financial, reputational, practical, relational and/or emotional risks of doing so – perhaps particularly if your reasons for leaving are potentially contentious.

> "I find it tragic that able leaders who fall dramatically from grace often share a common experience: their closest followers have long been aware of their fatal flaw and were unsuccessful in getting the leader to deal with it"
>
> Ira Chaleff in 'The Courageous Follower'[104]

The best tactics will vary depending on which of these situations you're facing and the personalities of the people involved, as well as your own traits and ways of working and of managing relationships. So, the following are purely examples for you to adapt and evolve bearing all of those things in mind[105].

- Focus your comments on explicit, specific behaviours, policies or data and their impact, *not on personality traits or critique of their character.*

- Unless you have very sound reasons to do otherwise, make it clear throughout that this is not a challenge to the leader's *authority.* Otherwise, you risk them or others interpreting your challenge as insubordination.

- Draw on your sense of authenticity and responsibility and make these explicit. When we focus on being authentic, we draw on our values and our aspirations to be the best person we can be *and* we check that the challenge we're keen to bring is truly objective, not rooted in our own baggage or agenda. When we draw on our sense of responsibility, we focus on a 'higher purpose' than ourselves or our own agendas, attending instead to the greater good, the shared endeavour, the need to role-model good followership to others or live up to others' expectations of us. When our leaders know we're challenging them out of a sense of duty, not a personal agenda, they're much more likely to listen to what we have to say – particularly if we've a proven track record of taking responsibility for collective success.

- Acknowledge the positives in their approach, intent and/or track record – and not in some lazy, transparent, unsubstantiated or sycophantic 'feedback sandwich'. For example, you might say "We really need your passion, clarity and confidence, Sarah. We're facing some tough times and you help keep us moving forward. Sometimes, though, it feels like you get carried away. Like yesterday: you spoke over people and didn't take time to listen to their ideas and concerns. Sure, we don't always have time for a huge discussion, but yesterday you ran the risk of people misreading your confidence as arrogance. They could easily have interpreted the fast pace, passion and focus as an attempt to rail-road us into doing something we don't fully believe in."

- Listen to the other party (or parties), assuming they have good intentions, however hard that might be, and try to understand the causes of their current approach. This doesn't mean you agree with them, sanction any inappropriate behaviours or accept that they'll continue – most of the leaders I've worked with do want challenge from their followers, but also want to be simultaneously respected and listened to.

- Paint a clear picture of the 'desired future state' and the benefits of achieving it – even better, vividly contrast this with the long-term impact of persisting with the current way of doing things.

- Be prepared to admit when you're wrong.

- Take responsibility for the potential downsides of your courageous action and, where appropriate, seek ways to limit the impact on others.

- Try indirect approaches where direct approaches trigger defensiveness. Chaleff offers a number of examples, including "How might [stakeholder X] interpret that?" and "What other plausible interpretations could there be?"[106]

- Seek allies to help boost and maintain your own courage. As well as building our confidence by agreeing with our views, encouraging us to share them and adding their own voices to ours, allies can help us secure a power base that reduces the probability or potency of any implicit or explicit threats being made against us. As Alan Murray notes in the *Wall Street Journal*, senior figures in organisations "are on shorter leashes, more beholden" to others than ever before[107]. Their positions may be more precarious as a result, but they do still have the power to influence our careers and broader lives. In addition, that precariousness and the vulnerability it brings will probably make them *more* sensitive to feeling betrayed and *more* likely to lash out if they do, not less. Also, when seeking allies, a great text called *Adaptive Leadership*[108] advises us to build alliances with resistors and potential resistors.

- Importantly, make going outside of the organisation your last resort: each time we expand the 'circle' of people who know about the wrongdoing, we increase the sense of betrayal and embarrassment felt by those at the centre. That in turn is likely to increase the perpetrators' fear, defensiveness and aggression, locking them into a pattern of behaviour that'll make it harder and harder for them to change. So, before you seek the outside influence of Alan Murray's "regulators, accountants, attorneys general, hedge-fund managers, union bosses, proxy-advisory services, trial lawyers, public pension funds and nonprofit activists"[109], make sure you've exhausted the options within your relationship with your boss, within the team, the department and the wider organisation.

- If it comes to leaving the team or organisation, think long and hard about whether you leave quietly, publicly renounce the leader or go further and actively oppose them from the 'outside'. You might find Lessons 3 ('Challenge your assumptions') and 4 ('We get the leader we deserve') in this book helpful when making this decision.

One final thing to remember when using any of these tactics (or others) to muster courage in the moment: if your courage is a short-term flash that quickly fades and you're seen not to stand by your convictions for the longer term, then it could potentially backfire on you and/or negatively affect the morale of people who're relying on you – whether that reliance is in practical terms or purely as a role model. So, be sure to factor that in when you're feeling the fear but are determined to "do it anyway".

In what ways (or on what topics) could you be more courageous in your relationship with your boss? For each thing you come up with, what's currently stopping you?

Drawing on the strategies and tactics in this book, as well as your own thinking on the subject, when you look at your responses to the previous question, what could you do to reduce the fear and/or do it anyway?

....

....

....

....

....

....

A note on whistleblowing

Despite Sarbanes-Oxley and various nations' whistleblowing legislation, the harsh reality is that the morally courageous act of whistleblowing often has a far-reaching and long-lasting negative impact on everyone involved. The whistleblower's career almost always suffers; their personal life is often disrupted and some face genuine financial hardship or threats of physical violence. Those left behind suffer, too, whether they were knowing participants in wrongdoing, tacitly complicit bystanders or blind to what was happening.

The best course of action, then, is to act as soon as possible: the longer we wait, the more opportunities there are for bad behaviour or bad practices to become habitual; the more those who are afraid to speak up will become complicit (and thus implicated) by their silence, so the more they'll have to lose if those bad behaviours or practices come to light.

Applying this lesson as a leader of others

Where are the people you lead on the 'commitment vs capacity' grid (below)?

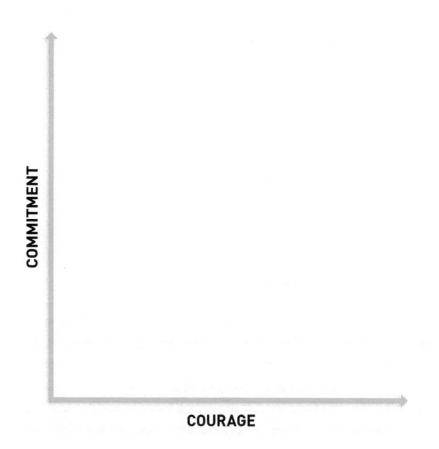

COURAGE

Who, if anyone, needs to move to somewhere else on the grid for the good of the team or organisation? What will it take to move them?

When you're challenging yourself to answer that last question, it's important to remember that it's easy to write off the passive resistors in the bottom left, to blame and chastise them for their lack of commitment. Better would be to find ways to help them be more courageous and air their grievances, concerns and any other reasons they're finding it hard to commit. After all, it's only by hearing them that you can address those obstacles to full commitment. Remember, too, that people in the bottom left are often particularly alert to risks and may have noticed things others haven't.

Rebels, too, are potential assets. Yes, they can destabilise the team and potentially the wider system, but instability also brings opportunity for insight and innovation. As with the passive resistors, the key is to resist judging and alienating them, to remember that people's commitment and courage will be affected by a range of different factors: the way you and their peers behave, for instance, the wider organisational context, events in their personal lives, and so on. So, in your role as their leader, and in leading the high-commitment lower-courage 'devotees' in your world, it's worth asking yourself (and them) "What am I doing to create a culture that breeds courage and rewards productive dissent?" After all, it's important to know that your hard-working 'devotees' are in the top left of the grid because they choose to be and not because they're scared to be anywhere else…

Courage and the minimum wage

Sylvie, the CEO of a business in a highly competitive market typically staffed by 'low skill' workers, employs several thousand people on the minimum wage in order to maintain a 5% profit margin.

When her mentor read an early draft of this book, he challenged the idea that she'd want those people to be courageous. "Authentic and responsible, yes," he said, "but the idea that Sylvie's staff will have the courage to challenge her misses the power and economic gap between shop floor and board room."

I'd challenge this on two levels: firstly, a culture that encourages them to challenge their bosses and the status quo from a trail-blazer perspective will be more likely to derive added value from them that'll help the company stay competitive. Secondly, this book focuses primarily on one's relationship with people one rung up the ladder. I'm not saying someone at the most junior level in an organisation should directly challenge someone on the board. I never said they shouldn't, either, but in doing so they'd be advised to do so responsibly and respectfully, taking heed of the other nine lessons in this book.

In summary

We've clarified what it means to be courageous at work, particularly in your relationship with your boss. We looked at three types of courageous action (moral, intellectual and aspirational) and you reflected on the extent to which you demonstrate and could further demonstrate each of the three with your boss.

We examined the relationship between courage and commitment, differentiating between passive resistors, rebels, devotees and trail-blazers – and you'll have considered which of those best describes you. Then I offered you three strategies for strengthening your base level of courage and a number of tactics to help you muster additional courage in the moment.

● ● ●

Lesson 10:
Promote and enable good followership in others

● ● ●

- Why you and your boss will thrive by promoting these lessons in others

- What are you and your boss role-modelling for others?

- How can you create a culture that recognises and rewards the habits and mind-sets at the heart of this book?

- How to select, enable and encourage people who create genuine, mutual value in their relationship with their boss

REMEMBER THAT business school professor I told you about in the introduction to this book, who belittled the role of good 'followership' to a group of fifty senior managers, all of whom were both leaders and followers? I strongly encourage you *not* to make the same mistake. If you're delivering on the first nine lessons in this book, then you *are* being a good follower – not in the passive, derogatory sense of the word, but as someone who's proactive, self-aware

> "When there are no good role models, become one"

> Gale Ann Hurd,[110]
> Film producer

and challenging; someone who's fully committed and takes responsibility, who's always on a learning curve; someone with a vision of their own and who expects a lot from their boss while understanding that their boss is just another human being with all the flaws and challenges that brings.

So far, the focus of this book has been very much on the relationship between you and your boss(es). If you're a leader in your own right, you'll also have been thinking about the relationships you have with the people you lead. As we begin this tenth and final lesson, we need to broaden that thinking. We need to be thinking about your peers and other people in your organisation. We need to be paying attention to the wider 'ecosystem' in which you work.

If you've acted on your thoughts and insights from the first nine lessons and shared some of that thinking with your boss(es), then I believe they'll be feeling the benefits. If they are, then I'd expect them to be acting as an enabling force – rather than a blocker – when it comes to you thriving in your role. Your relationship with them should be (even) stronger, more enjoyable and more effective. Not only that, but the actions you'll have taken and the changes you'll have started to make should force or encourage them to make positive changes to the way they lead – and you'll be making it easier for them to do so.

If you've changed your approach to working with your boss, you'll also be making it easier for your colleagues to do the same. You'll have raised your boss's expectations of everyone they lead, which will encourage your boss to encourage everyone to raise their game. If you've openly discussed your experience and/or this book with your boss's direct reports, then you'll have given them a head-start when it comes to meeting your boss's elevated expectations. You'll have laid the foundations for improving the way the whole team operates.

If you've shared these lessons more widely, with colleagues across the organisation, then you'll have contributed to a potential shift in the way a whole tier in the hierarchy operates, influencing a whole cohort's views of what it means to have a truly effective relationship with one's boss; what it really means to lead; and what it takes to operate as a high performing team.

If you're a leader, then promoting the lessons in this book to those who follow you is another way to improve the culture and performance of your team and of the whole organisation. Share these lessons with the people you lead and they'll expect *and* enable you to be an even better leader. By stepping up in their own right, they'll be freeing you up to take on greater, more complex and rewarding challenges. That might mean promotion; it might not. It might have nothing to do with status and pay rises, and be purely about keeping your working life fresh and interesting.

Encouraging your peers and direct reports to take this essential relationship seriously will also serve to enhance the collective value you deliver to your organisation and its stakeholders, and will make life easier for you. It's far easier to change the way we do things – or even to change our mind-set – when we're doing so with the support of our peers and the people we lead.

If you commit to the effort required to deliver on the first nine lessons but don't involve your colleagues in a discussion of the virtues and nature of high-quality followership, they might even get in your way. It'll be easier for them to misinterpret the change, to become jealous, or confused, or cynical, or even to feel threatened. Think of them as the 'immune system' around you, into which you're introducing a foreign cell. Unless you can convince that immune system that it's a friendly cell then that immune system will treat those new behaviours as a threat, a virus that needs to be fought with all the tools at its disposal.

There's another important benefit to promoting and enabling good followership in others: most of us learn well by teaching others. By engaging in the debate, by discussing what we've learned – whether it's from this book or elsewhere – we enrich and embed our own learning, which increases our chances of making a significant, sustained change to the way we operate.

In the way you 'follow' your boss

As well as sharing what you've learned with your boss and peers, you'll be promoting good followership every time you role-model the lessons in this book. People will see it in the ways you show that you value the act of following as much as the act of leading – that you aspire to being a great follower, rather than denigrating followership as some weak, pitiful, subservient or less valuable opposite of leadership. Your bosses and colleagues will experience the passion you feel when you've chosen to align yourself with a leader who enables you and your team mates to fulfil your own vision (from Lesson 1) while delivering exceptional value to the team and organisation. They'll better appreciate that they, too, can choose consciously which leaders to follow and which to avoid (as in Lesson 2). At the same time, they'll recognise that – in many ways – we set our leaders up to fail and unintentionally sabotage their efforts to do otherwise (Lessons 3 and 4).

They'll see you and your team benefiting from getting greater clarity from your boss and other stakeholders (Lesson 5). They'll hear you spoken about as someone who takes due responsibility and seeks out more, without invading others' territory or putting your own needs above anyone else's (Lesson 6). They'll be inspired – or intimidated – by your focus on continuous self-improvement and the attention you pay to building the capacity of the teams and organisation in which you work (covered in Lesson 7). They'll admire your exemplary commitment and the way you secure commitment from others (Lesson 8). They'll each benefit differently from each of your acts of courage (Lesson 9): for some you'll be a role model, catalyst or rallying point; for others an ally providing additional momentum to their own existing acts of bravery; to others you'll be an adversary inviting them to step up and truly be heard.

In some cases, role modelling is enough. In others, you'll realise there's more you can do to enable those around you. For each of the lessons in this book, it's worth asking "What can I do to help my colleagues engage with this idea and find their own way to deliver on it?" For example:

- When you're listening to someone complaining about their boss, how can you use what you learned in Lesson 3 ('Challenge your assumptions') and Lesson 4 ('We get the leader we deserve') to help them reframe their situation and find a more productive way forward, rather than leaving them with a 'victim' mentality?

- How might you use Lesson 5 ('Seek clarity') to help them gain the clarity they need to launch a complex project, or get one back on track? And how can you draw on Lesson 7 ('Build capacity') to help them ensure the right processes are in place to facilitate efficient, effective communication, knowledge-sharing and decision-making from start to finish?

- What can you take from Lesson 6 ('Take due responsibility') and Lesson 7 ('Continually build your capacity') to help a colleague find or build sufficient capacity to redistribute responsibilities in their area and/or take on greater, more rewarding responsibilities of their own?

- How can you use the framework in Lesson 6 to increase levels of trust across your team or department, rather than simply in your own relationships?

- How can you use the learning in Lesson 8 ('Secure and maintain commitment') to make it *easier* for your colleagues to secure and maintain your commitment, as well as their own and that of their key stakeholders? It's understandably tempting to resist others' attempts to influence us, but what if you focused instead on making it *easier* for them to understand the less obvious needs they'll have to meet if they're to get you fully on-board?

- How can you draw on Lesson 9 ('Be courageous') to facilitate more courageous interactions between you and your peers, and between your peers and your boss?

- How can you draw on Lessons 6, 8 and 9 to increase the team's sense of shared responsibility for a higher purpose, overcome the tendency to work in silos and reduce the temptation to vie for the boss's favour?

In your role as a leader

If you have leadership responsibilities of your own, then the way you work with your boss will set the tone for your relationships with the people you lead. If you change the way you 'follow' your boss, your people might well notice you role-modelling the change you want to see in them.

I see three spheres of influence through which you can promote effective followership: selecting, equipping and encouraging.

Selecting

All too often, recruitment focuses exclusively or almost exclusively on technical skills and how much experience a person has of doing the very same job in the past. Where the role includes leading others, most recruiters pay considerable attention to the candidate's ability to lead; rarely is due care given to a candidate's ability to create value in the role of follower.

Interviews are still the most commonly used tool in selection. Many are conducted badly and risk adding no further intelligence than that provided by a good CV. Many interviewers crash in with leading questions, don't listen to answers and fail to probe beyond superficial responses and bluffs. Done well, though – and despite claims to the contrary – they are still among the most effective methods available[111].

If you're looking for someone who's going to build a good relationship with their boss and other senior figures, it's worth asking them at least some of the following questions. Where there's more than one question per bullet, the additional ones are meant as follow-up questions.

- Tell me about the best relationship you've had with a boss. What did they bring to that relationship? What did you bring?

- No matter how senior we are, all of us follow someone. What qualities do you think make for a good follower?

- What do you need from the people who lead you? Tell me about a time when you didn't get those things. What effect did it have on you? How did it impact your work? What did you do about it?

- Tell me about your last / current boss. What drives them? Who are / were their key stakeholders? What did those people expect from your boss? How does your boss prefer to communicate? What approach do they take to making decisions? What are their key strengths? What unhelpful habits do they have? How are those triggered? What was your contribution to helping them channel their strengths and avoid falling foul of their bad habits and weaknesses?

- What things have you taken on in previous roles that were beyond your official remit? How did people respond? How did you balance those additional responsibilities with your existing workload? What was the long-term impact?

- Tell me about a time when you disagreed with your boss. How did you deal with that situation? How did they respond to you? What was the outcome?

- Tell me about a time when your loyalty to your boss was tested. What made you loyal to them in the first place? How did you respond to the situation? What was the outcome (for you, for them, for others)?

- Tell me about a time when you or others felt your boss was underperforming or not doing their job as well as they could. What did you do? What was the impact?

There are other questions you could ask, of course. Each of the lessons in this book offers inspiration. I've tried to avoid questions you'd probably be asking anyway.

If you're using personality questionnaires, measures of emotional intelligence, reference checks and/or assessment centre exercises to vet your candidates, then I'd encourage you to look for what those tell you about the likely answers to the questions above and for other signs that your candidates are living up to – or show the potential to live up to – the first nine lessons in this book.

Enabling

As leaders, it's important to ask ourselves how well we're enabling others to follow us. For each lesson in this book, there are important questions we should be asking about our relationships with each of the people we lead. For example:

- What training and development do we offer that educates people at all levels of seniority on the value and nature of good followership?

- To what extent are we helping people to clarify their own aspirations and to find a way to make progress on them (Lesson 1)?

- Are we taking sufficient responsibility for being the kind of leaders people would *want* to follow (Lesson 2) or are we continually underperforming in that regard as leaders, or making them feel like they don't have much choice but to follow?

- How well are we helping our followers understand and challenge the assumptions and expectations they bring to relationships with their bosses (Lesson 3)?

- How effectively are we raising people's awareness of the interactions between their own needs and those of their boss (Lesson 4)? To what extent are we addressing the potential for unmet needs to derail that relationship and both parties' performance?

- How much clarity do we give people when establishing objectives and delegating authority (Lesson 5)? And how much do we avoid giving that clarity because of our own habits, preferences, needs, fears and expectations?

- How effectively do we enable our people to take responsibility and build their own capacity (Lessons 6 and 7)?

- What skills, training, processes and resources do we have in place to help them secure and maintain buy-in from their (and our) key stakeholders (Lesson 8)?

- What more could we be doing to build the skills, confidence, resources and processes required for people to be more courageous (Lesson 9) and to create a team and organisational climate that promotes courage in those that follow us?

Feel free to use the space below to record your own initial responses to the questions above or to craft questions of your own.

All of these are questions to explore one-to-one and/or with the team as a whole – if you've the courage to do so! If you do, I'd suggest framing these as questions that ask about the dynamic in your relationship with them and in their relationships with each other. For example, for Lesson 5 ('Seek clarity'), "How effectively do we ensure everyone in the team has sufficient clarity to enable them to do their job to the best of their ability?" That is, make them questions that invite self-reflection from everyone, including you, and honest feedback that's about *the team* (including you) – rather than questions that focus all responsibility on you as the team leader. You have a part to play, for sure, and you have a disproportionate influence on the culture of the team, but this shouldn't (just) be about you changing the way you operate. At the same time, if you leave it all to them, you're ignoring the fact that you're likely to be one of the key blockers or enablers to their ability, and desire, to follow you well.

Encouraging

If 'exceptional followership' is the direction you're keen to head in and 'enabling' is the capacity-building that'll help you get there, then 'encouraging' is the carrot and stick that secure and maintain people's commitment to raising the bar. As with all encouragement, it starts with employee attraction, recruitment, selection and on-boarding: the clearer the messages from the start, the greater the influence on people's behaviours once they're part of the team.

After that, as we've seen, commitment relies on trust and a willingness to challenge suboptimal behaviours and hold people accountable for following well. This means recognising and rewarding those who demonstrate good followership as well as imposing sanctions on those who don't. Agreeing the nature of those sanctions isn't going to be easy. Neither is one of the biggest changes we'll need to make if we're going to create the kind of cultural shift required to truly embed respect for high-quality followership: we're going to need to make following well a prerequisite for promotion into leadership positions. After all, leaders who can't follow are liabilities: they're more likely to have dysfunctional relationships with their own superiors, which is likely to create unnecessary, unproductive tension and problems for their staff and stakeholders.

Again, each lesson in this book draws our attention to important questions when it comes to encouraging our people to follow well.

- What stories are we telling that show that we place great value on good followership – perhaps even as much value as we place on good leadership?

- How hard do we work to ensure sufficient alignment between the team's / organisation's needs and the aspirations, needs and motivations of team members (echoing Lessons 1 and 8)?

- How well do we encourage and reward upwards feedback (Lesson 2), self-awareness and the ability to *really* understand others (Lessons 3 and 4)?

- How do we react when our direct reports seek additional clarity from us (Lesson 5)?

- How effectively do we reward those who take on additional responsibility, and how well do we discourage territorialism and the avoidance of responsibility (Lesson 6)?

- How explicitly do we reward those who continually improve themselves and their environment and discourage those who are coasting or making no contribution to enhancing the team's / organisation's capacity (Lesson 7)?

- What expectations are we communicating – explicitly and covertly, consciously and unintentionally – when it comes to moral, intellectual and aspirational courage in our team and organisation (Lesson 9)?

I've used "we" intentionally when framing all of these questions. This isn't just about what you're doing as an individual leader: it's about what your staff are doing, and what their staff are doing if they have any. It's about the ways your peers and the people above you are encouraging, reinforcing and/or discouraging good followership – and they could be doing all three at once. It's also about the nature of your team's relationships with their other stakeholders. So, whenever you're looking at one of those 'we' questions above, you'll get most value if you're able to think of the whole ecosystem, rather than just yourself or you and one direct report.

As before, these are questions you can ask usefully of yourself as we come to the end of this book, but they're also questions you can use in one-to-one conversations with team members and/or with the whole team. You might even consider weaving these questions into your appraisal discussions, as an alternative to traditional and rather turgid ratings and competencies. In whatever context you choose to use them, I'd suggest adopting the same approach I recommended under 'enabling' earlier in this lesson.

Feel free to use the space below for your initial responses to the questions above, or for questions of your own.

In summary

In this final lesson, we've shifted the focus from you and your boss to the wider team and organisation, arguing that you'll achieve much more for yourself and your boss if you're able to encourage others to step up when it comes to the first nine lessons in this book. There are two ways to do so:

1. Role-modelling those nine lessons yourself

2. As a leader, creating the right conditions for great followership.

The latter means selecting people who are likely to live up to the nine lessons, then enabling and encouraging them to do so.

• ● •

Bringing it all together

•●•

- What we've covered

- What you've learned

- What you're doing differently

- Where to from here?

THE TEN LESSONS IN THIS BOOK cover a lot of ground.
Frankly, with so little written on this topic, they needed to. I'm certainly not
expecting you to remember all ten off the top of your head. You will find
the underlying framework helpful, though: those Three Core Disciplines
and the ARC Qualities.

The ARC qualities – being Authentic, Responsible and Courageous
– help us channel our habits, needs and mind-sets (and those of others)
in ways that make it easier
to deliver on the Three Core
Disciplines. When we attend
responsibly to our own needs
and others', for example, we're
more likely to head in a
direction that'll secure the
commitment of everyone involved. When we're Authentic
and Courageous, we'll challenge the limitations of our
existing habits and mind-sets

and those of others. This in turn increases our capacity to deliver and opens our eyes to ever bolder, more creative directions to head in and ways to get there.

Each of the ten lessons draws on one or more of the Three Core Disciplines and ARC Qualities. Each seeks to raise awareness of your existing mind-set, your current habits and the needs that underpin the relationship between you and your boss.

The ten lessons in brief – and how well you're living up to them

If you've been working through the questions in each of the ten lessons in this book, then you'll have a pretty good indication already of the kind (and calibre) of relationship you've built with your past and present bosses. If you're a leader, your thinking will have informed the way you lead and the culture you've created around you that make it easier, or harder, for the people you lead to build healthy, mutually beneficial relationships with you.

To help you focus your efforts going forward, I recommend using the following summary as a means of assessing how well you think you're living up to each of the ten lessons, by rating yourself and seeking qualitative feedback from your boss and/or others.

Personally, I'd like to see those kinds of feedback conversations either integrated into or taking the place of traditional performance management processes. The annual, ratings-based performance appraisal is a tired old beast that needs replacing with a conversation that's more interesting, helpful, tangible and motivating.

Lesson summary	The big question	Your response (a rating from 0-10)
Lesson 1: **Have a vision of your own** Having a vision of our own keeps us more motivated, enhances our resilience and improves satisfaction with our jobs and lives. A vision acts as a focal point, guiding us through difficult times and decisions, and helping us measure our progress. If you've used the tools I've offered, you'll have a clear, compelling statement of intent that's been thoroughly tested and backed up with clear actions to get you started. You'll also have some allies to help you turn that vision into reality.	How clear, authentic, responsible and courageous is your vision for what you want to achieve in your career and what you want to contribute?	
Lesson 2: **Choose your leader wisely** Many of us feel we can't choose our leader. However, when you're looking at a new job or boss, I'd encourage you to really do your homework before you commit to the relationship. Take time to clarify up front what you and they will need and how you'll need to adapt to create maximum value in the relationship. If you invested in this lesson, you should have a clear picture of the kind of leader you're looking for and the extent to which those above and around you are the right leaders for you.	How consciously and wisely have you chosen your current boss?	

Lesson summary	The big question	Your response (a rating from 0-10)
Lesson 3: *Challenge your assumptions* We considered the ways in which your assumptions and expectations around leadership, relationships and the world in general might be setting your leader up to disappoint you. You had the opportunity to dig deep, to challenge your existing perspectives and their implications and make changes that'll strengthen the foundations of any relationship you have with current and future bosses.	To what extent are your own expectations and assumptions about leadership, relationships and the world around you making it easier for your boss to give you what you need?	
Lesson 4: *We get the leader we deserve* We looked at three fundamental human needs (inclusion, control and affection) and the role these play in your relationship with your boss. You'll have questioned the extent to which your desire to get those needs met is helping and hindering your relationship with your boss.	How aware are you of the impact of your needs – and any conflicts between your needs and your boss's needs – on your relationship with your boss?	

Lesson summary	The big question	Your response (a rating from 0-10)
Lesson 5: *Seek clarity* How can you ever truly deliver if you don't know what your boss really wants? In this lesson, we explored a Five-Phase Framework for clarifying our bosses' true needs, aspirations and concerns: first engage, then assess, then align, progress and review. We also looked at 'seven levels of delegation' as a tool for clarifying degrees of autonomy.	How clear are you and your boss regarding what each of you expects of the other and the degree of autonomy and authority you have?	
Lesson 6: *Take due responsibility* We tackled the pros and cons of taking additional responsibility – the former including enhanced performance, productivity, profitability, team cohesion, development, career progression, status, power and the accumulation of others' trust, respect and gratitude. You'll have decided what you can (and shouldn't) take additional responsibility for, and the levers you might need to pull to get your boss to trust you enough to *let* you take that responsibility on.	How broadly and effectively have you adopted additional responsibility beyond your stated remit?	

Lesson summary	The big question	Your response (a rating from 0-10)
Lesson 7: *Continually build your capacity* Without sufficient capacity, you'll really struggle to deliver, which is bad for you and your boss and – in a fast-moving world – if you don't continually build your capacity you'll be left behind. The questions posed in this lesson will have helped you get a clearer view of the additional skills, knowledge and resources you'll need to succeed, the process improvements you can make and ways to work more effectively with the organisational structures in which you operate.	How consistently, proactively and effectively have you been securing and developing the knowledge, skills, resources and processes (in *and* around you) that you'll need to succeed?	
Lesson 8: *Secure and maintain commitment* Without commitment, a clear direction and the necessary capacity will only take you so far. So this lesson used the Three Core Disciplines and the three ARC Qualities to help you understand what causes your own commitment, your boss's commitment and the commitment of your key stakeholders to wax and wane over time. You'll have assessed your boss's and others' current commitment and identified ways to boost it where necessary.	How effectively and proactively are you maintaining your own commitment *and* that of your boss?	

Lesson summary	The big question	Your response (a rating from 0-10)
Lesson 9: **Be courageous** In this lesson, you'll have considered what it means to be courageous at work, particularly in your relationship with your boss, using three types of courageous action (moral, intellectual and aspirational) as your guide. You'll have placed yourself and others on a grid pitting courage against commitment, asking whether you and they are currently 'passive resistors', 'rebels', 'devotees' or 'trail-blazers'.	How courageous are you being in your relationship with your boss?	
Lesson 10: **Promote and enable good followership** You'll achieve much more for yourself and your boss if you're able to help others live up to the first nine lessons in this book. It's a start to simply role-model those lessons yourself, but you'll contribute a lot more if you work on creating the right conditions for great followership in others. Lesson 10 offers a number of pointers for selecting people who are likely to live up to the nine lessons, as well as ways to enable and encourage them (and others) to do so.	To what extent are you actively promoting good followership in the people around you (by role-modelling it and by selecting, enabling and encouraging others)?	

Where you see room for improvement, what practical steps are you going to take to improve things? What conversations might that require, and who could you call on to hold you to account?

....

....

....

....

Where to from here?

You may have noticed already that there's a chapter that follows this one. It's intended for you to read in about three months' time. The road to Hell, they say, is paved with good intentions, and there are many books that sell well and read well but gather dust without ever truly changing the way their readers think and operate. I've done what I can to make this book interactive and practical, but the real value will come from you and whether you actually put these lessons into practice. Making a commitment to come back will help.

Other readers have asked what I'd recommend to leaders, teams and organisations. For leaders, I've responded by adding tips at the end of each lesson as to how to apply that lesson with the people they lead, and I believe Lesson 10 offers a lot of further thinking when it comes to creating the kind of culture that will support and encourage people to take these ten lessons on board. If you're looking for more in your capacity as a leader, then it would be remiss of me not to mention my previous book *ARC Leadership: from surviving to thriving in a complex world*. I believe leaders who are 'authentic, responsible and courageous' are better to work for and will make a more powerful positive contribution to their organisations and the wider world. They're also more likely to create the conditions in which the people they lead can deliver on the ten lessons you and I have explored here.

Where teams are concerned, I *am* planning to write a book for teams to read together. Like this book, it'll build on my previous work without relying on it. For now, I'd encourage teams to use these ten lessons as a conversation piece – to ask each other the questions I've posed and to challenge themselves and each other to come up with new questions inspired by each of the lessons. I'd also encourage teams to use the underlying framework: the Three Core Disciplines; the idea of habits, needs and mind-sets helping or hindering teams' ability to deliver on those Core Disciplines; the role of the ARC Qualities in helping turn those habits, needs and mind-sets into enablers rather than obstacles.

"How are our current ways of looking at the world, our expectations and assumptions, limiting our thinking about the future direction of this team?" is a helpful question, for example. It draws explicitly on just two of those ingredients (mind-set and direction) but is also a call on the team to take an honest, authentic look at its ways of thinking, to take responsibility for the ways in which it's limiting itself, and perhaps to be courageous enough to challenge and change its existing world view.

Where organisations are concerned, I'd love to meet management teams, HR Directors or heads of Learning and Development who have the courage to commission a followership development programme – if only just to wave it in the face of the business school professor whose story I told at the start of this book. When I started writing *The Boss Factor*, I thought that highly unlikely – after all, the term 'follower' feels too heavily laden with negative connotations. But a programme that looks specifically at the relationship between people and their bosses, looking up rather than down? That feels important and sorely lacking.

It seems a number of people and organisations agree with me. Some have asked for additional support to accompany this book – one-to-ones, webinars or physical drop-in sessions focusing on particular lessons, where they can discuss the various questions and challenges with like-minded people from their own or other organisations. Some have asked about formal training courses or commissioned sessions on the topic. I can see pros and cons of each approach, so if you think they're onto something or you've other ideas, get in touch.

In conclusion

When I set out to write this book, I wanted to offer something practical, accessible and perhaps even inspiring to people at all levels who – in a world obsessed with leaders and leadership – have had precious little support when it comes to managing the relationship with those who lead *them*. I'm hoping I've achieved that.

As we bring this book to a close, until you return in three months' time, I'd encourage you to reflect on the impact you and your boss have on each other's lives. I imagine, like most people, you talk about your boss to others – your colleagues, people you lead, your friends, your family. No doubt they'll also be talking about you. Depending on the nature of that relationship, and all the relationships around it, the two of you might be telling those people how much you like each other, how much you value that relationship, how you achieve so much more together than either of you could apart, how you learn from each other's successes and mistakes, and strengths and weaknesses. Or you could each be talking about how the other frustrates, disables and blocks you – ignoring your own failings or blaming them on the other, perhaps with you acting the child while they play the absent, weak or overbearing parent.

My hope is that you'll increasingly fall into the first camp – if you are not there already. I'm hoping you'll be truly authentic in this relationship – honest with yourself and developing upwards relationships that feel true to who you are and want to be. I'm hoping you'll take responsibility for your role in that relationship: for the baggage you're bringing into it from past relationships with authority figures; for the things you do that could trigger less-than-optimal behaviours in your boss; responsibility for making your boss as successful as you'd hope they want to make you; responsibility for helping them become a better leader. And I'm hoping you'll be genuinely and responsibly courageous: in challenging your boss; in standing up for them and your shared endeavour; in pushing yourself to get better and better at 'managing up for mutual gain'.

• ● •

Don't forget to come back in three months' time to review your progress, and do get in touch if you're stuck and need help, or simply want to share what you've taken from this book. You'll find my contact details at www.leaderspace.com.

For now, good luck, and remember that great Irish saying:

> "You'll never plough a field by turning it over in your mind"

Three months on

• ● •

- What's happened since you last picked up the book?

- What successes have you had?

- Where have you stalled or relapsed?

- How might you have used this book differently if, when you started, you knew the things you know now?

WELL DONE FOR RETURNING and welcome back! All too often, we finish books with good intentions but don't take the time to check if the learning has truly bedded in.

If it's been a while since you were here and your memory of the ten lessons is a little hazy, then you might benefit from a quick skim of the previous chapter, which summarises all ten. You might even re-score yourself against the questions that summary poses.

Whether the lessons are hazy or fresh, I'd recommend using the following questions to chart your progress over the past few weeks.

What's changed for you and your boss since you last picked up this book? Which of the ten lessons draw your attention now, as a result of that change / lack of change?

....

....

....

Which of the ten lessons have had the greatest impact on your relationship with your boss, and why?

Which lessons (if any) are you finding it hardest to live up to? What's getting in the way (think in terms of the obstacles within you as well as those around you)? And what help can you get to overcome those obstacles?

In retrospect, how might you have used this book differently if you'd known then what you know now?

....

....

....

....

....

Once again, I'm impressed that you've taken the time to check in on your progress. I hope this book and its lessons are continuing to bring you value and I hope your boss appreciates the effort you're putting in!

It'd be good to hear from you, even if it's just to share the most valuable nuggets you've taken from the time we've spent together.

All the best

Richard

● ● ●

Acknowledgements

• ● •

THEY'D NO IDEA at the time but it was Sarah Mast and Angela Gunn who accidentally created the creative conditions that triggered the thinking that eventually gave birth to this book. Sarah and Angela kindly invited me to play 'thought leader' and anchor-man for a global leadership programme at De Lage Landen in the Netherlands. It was on my way home, at Schipol airport in Amsterdam, that I came up with the idea for the book and scoped out the ten lessons on my phone.

I'd have neither had the idea nor been able to flesh out that initial sketch, though, if it wasn't for the hundreds of clients I've worked with over the years and the bosses, colleagues, researchers and other writers I've learned from along the way. Where the theory and academic rigour are concerned, Ira Chaleff, Karen Ellis, Robert Hogan, Barbara Kellerman, Robert E Kelley, David Rooke, Will Schutz, Sabina Spencer and Bill Torbert have been particularly influential in helping me shape my thinking on this particular topic. Anton Horne (the master connector) deserves a special mention, too, for hooking me into the Mission Command model that helped me shape Lesson 5. Greg Reed and Stella Pitt helped me get the facts straight regarding the HomeServe case studies offered in Lesson 6.

Even with all that material to work with, this book wouldn't be the book it is without the time, energy and enthusiastic critique given it by those who offered to read the first draft. In the UK: Andy Homer at Merryck and Co; Catherine Poyner at the Cabinet Office; Colin Clarkson-Short, Dave Tansley and Gary Semple; Geoff Morey and Neil Van Niekerk at Macmillan Cancer Support; Karen Butler; Michael Borthwick at Claranet; Peter Young; Rebecca Stevens; Seb Henkes, founder of Sabio; Simon

Haskey at Dell, Tim Patterson at Larkshead Media, Tony Cooper and Tony Wringe. In The Netherlands: Vicky Monsieurs at Philips. In Australia: Britta van Dyk and Mary Donnelly-Wells. In the USA: Dr Krister Lowe at The Team Coaching Zone, and Mark Griffiths who's been reading my work for decades. The dozens of pages of comments, critique and suggestions they offered have made a fantastic difference to this book, for which I'm hugely grateful.

And then there's the crew who turned my scrappy-looking text and images into the highly-polished and aesthetically-pleasing product you have before you: editor Jackie King, layout-meister Alison Rayner, graphics aficionado and cover designer Jeff Fuge, and proof-reader Jenni Boston (who also led me through my first 20-odd years on this planet as my long-suffering mother and for whom I was probably not the model follower). Thanks, too, to my publicists Katie Read and Katherine Lowe at READ Media. Katie, Katherine, Ali and Jeff also went above and beyond to come to my aid at the eleventh hour when we needed to get very creative very quickly in the face of a whole ton of deadlines! For the same reasons, I'm also very grateful to Karen Ellis and Chris Haywood.

Finally, there's my wife Jane: given the impact of my work on our home life over the years, and my tendency to take writing time during the school holidays, I made it my mission to try to write this book without her noticing. I managed to keep it under the radar for quite some time, but didn't quite live up to that aspiration. I'm hoping the impact has been minimal and I'm grateful for her never-ending tolerance of my passion for writing and my addiction to a vocation that has become her profession, too.

● ● ●

About the author

∙ ● ∙

RICHARD BOSTON
is a father, husband and keen runner. He's also a psychologist specialising in leadership and team performance. In that capacity, he coaches individuals and teams and develops leadership programmes for a diverse range of organisations. His work has taken him to six continents on behalf of clients like Cancer Research, Deloitte, GSK, Gucci, Heineken, Nickelodeon, Santander, Siemens, Shell, the South Australian Government, Southampton Football Club, Virgin and the UK's central government, health service and armed forces.

He is founder and Managing Director of his own consultancy firm, has acted as external faculty for select business schools, including Oxford-Saïd, London Business School and Trinity College Dublin, and was the lead author of Henley Business School's 2013 paper on the future of leadership development. He wrote his first book, *ARC Leadership: from surviving to thriving in a complex world*, in a bid to encourage leaders to be more Authentic, Responsible and Courageous to help turn back the rising tide of mistrust in leadership in all sectors. He also writes for magazines, blogs on LinkedIn, enjoys writing fiction and is currently exploring the implications for leadership of developments in artificial intelligence.

You'll find him, his work and more of his writing on LinkedIn, at www.leaderspace.com and occasionally on Twitter at @rejboston, or you can contact him via publications@leaderspace.com.

∙ ● ∙

References and notes

• ● •

1. From page 243 of B. Kellerman (2008) Followership: how followers are creating change and changing leaders. Boston, Mass: Harvard Business Press.

2. A fairly vast body of research exists highlighting a number of factors that drive stress in the workplace, including the degree of autonomy we have in our work, role clarity, the quality of our relationships, the support we receive and the amount of control we have over the volume and pace of our work. All of these are positively influenced by the 10 lessons in this book. If you'd like to read more, a good starting point is http://www.hse.gov.uk/stress/furtheradvice/causesofstress.htm

3. Lack of followership development is cited as a contributor to the air force's failure to meet targets for the staff retention and tenure in Lt Col S. M. Latour & Lt Col V. J. Rast (2004) Dynamic Followership: The Prerequisite for Effective Leadership. *Air and Space Power Journal, Winter.* Retrieved from http://govleaders.org/dynamicfollowership.htm on 17 Oct 2016.

4. R. Boston (2014) *ARC Leadership: from surviving to thriving in a complex world.* London: LeaderSpace.

5. These cultural comparisons are based on the model pioneered by Geert Hofstede. See, for instance, G. Hofstede (2001) *Culture's Consequences: comparing values, behaviors, institutions, and organizations across nations. (2nd ed.)* Thousand Oaks, CA: SAGE Publications.

6. Quoted by D. Blagg and S. Young (2001) What Makes A Good Leader. *Harvard Alumni Stories,* 1 Feb. Retrieved from https://www.alumni.hbs.edu/stories/Pages/story-bulletin.aspx?num=3059 on 29 June 2017.

7. The research in question followed nearly 5000 people over 7-10 years and found that those assessed as having a sense of purpose at the outset earned more and accumulated more. The effect was stronger for those aged 20-35 than for older participants, perhaps because those older than 35 had already accumulated much of their wealth. As Christian Jarrett at *The Psychologist* commented, it would be good to know whether certain visions are more associated with higher income generation than others, but the researchers didn't look into that. The original research paper is P. L. Hill, N. A. Turiano, D. K. Mroczek & A. L. Burrow (2016) The Value of a Purposeful Life: sense of purpose predicts greater

income and net worth. *Journal of Research in Personality, 65,* pp38-42. Christian's comments are at https://digest.bps.org.uk/2016/12/31/find-a-sense-of-purpose-and-youre-more-likely-to-get-rich/ (retrieved on 29 June 2017).

8.　See　https://developingpeople.org/2017/01/01/why-many-of-us-lack-any-vision-for-our-lives-happy-new-year/ (retrieved on 29 June 2017).

9.　I've tried searching for the original source, but I've been unable to find it. If you have better luck, please let me know

10.　Based on a survey of 514 employees who were 'new starters' (those who started a new job in the previous 12 months) and 1134 line managers of new starters. Ninety two per cent worked full time, 54% in the private sector, 30% in the public sector and 16% in the third sector. See Institute of Leadership & Management (2016) *Beyond the Honeymoon: keeping new employees from the exits.* Available from www.InstituteLM.com/resourceLibrary/BeyondtheHoneymoon.html retrieved on 29 June 2017).

11.　*Ibid.*

12.　*Ibid.*

13.　The same source found that in the business services industry 65.7% of new employees leave within a year – understandable given the high proportion of temporary workers. Voluntary turnover in the first year is still high, though, in transportation (over 50%), the information sector (around 43%), financial services (37.5%) and health care (nearly 37%). See A. Vaccaro (2014) Why Employees Quit Jobs Right After They've Started. *Inc, 17 April.* Retrieved from http://www.inc.com/adam-vaccaro/voluntary-turnover-six-months.html on 29 June 2017.

14.　The irony here is that the actual research is less conclusive but the headline continues all the same. From my perspective, virtually everything else that emerges in the 'Top 5 reasons' research, though, is something that is determined by the person's manager or heavily influenced by it. So, when we include its direct effects and its indirect effects, that relationship between a person and their boss is a massive contributor to people's tenure in organisations. It's also worth noting that there's research suggesting that people leave good bosses almost as frequently as they leave bad bosses, just for healthier reasons. See, for instance, R. S. Gajendran & D. Somaya (2016) Employees Leave Good Bosses Nearly as Often as Bad Ones. *Harvard Business Review,* 8 March. Retrieved from- https://hbr.org/2016/03/employees-leave-good-bosses-nearly-as-often-as-bad-ones&ab=Article-Links-End_of_Page_Recirculation on 29 June 2017.

15.　If you'd like to learn more from Hogan's perspective, a good starting point is www.hoganassessments.com. You're also, of course, welcome to get in touch with me.

16. I'm referring here to Talent Q which produced its own material on derailers, which you can find at www.talentqgroup.com

17. Furnham, A., Hyde, G., & Trickey, G. (2013). Do Your Dark Side Traits Fit? Dysfunctional Personalities in Different Work Sectors. *Applied Psychology*. Retrieved from http://dx.doi.org/10.1111/apps.12002 on 29 June 2017.

18. Talent Q white paper (2010) *Personality and Leadership Derailment: exploring how the personality of an individual plays a key role in determining someone's likelihood of derailment*. Retrieved from https://www.talentqgroup.com/media/40489/ whitepaper-personality-leadership-derailment.pdf on 29 June 2017.

19. These trends were seen in people's Hogan Development Survey profiles across at least two studies. The first, with 18,366 British Adults (12,033 male and 6,333 female) you'll find in A. Furnham & G. Trickey (2011). Sex differences in dark side traits. Personality and Individual Differences, 50, 517-522. The second, with 4,943 British Adults (2,828 male and 2,115 female) is in A. Furnham, G. Trickey & G. Hyde (2012) Bright Aspects to dark side traits: Dark Side traits associated with work success. *Personality and Individual Differences, 52,* pp908-913.

20. D. L. Dotlich & P. C. Cairo (2003) *Why CEOs Fail*. San Francisco, CA: Jossey-Bass.

21. Chester Elton and his colleagues used a 100-question psychometric with 25,000 people, including more than 4,000 Millennials, aimed at ascertaining what motivates people at work. Of the 23 potential motivators in Elton and Co's list, the one that more than two thirds of Millennials prioritised was Impact – the sense of making a difference in the world and the belief that the work they're doing matters. We should, however, be wary of these kinds of self-report measures. What people say motivates them and what actually drives their behaviour on a day-to-day basis can differ enormously. The statistics on volunteering, for instance, show that younger people are less likely to offer their services for free to worthy causes than their elders. Yes, there are situational reasons why that might be the case, but consider too the charge that Millennials are self-centred and self-obsessed; that they have wider social circles but that those circles are actually pretty low in diversity because by casting a wider net it's easier to find more people who think, look and behave just like them. See, for example, C. Elton & A. Gostick (2017) *How making a difference in the world reduces employee turnover*. Retrieved from www.linkedin.com/pulse/

how-making-difference-world-reduces-employee-turnover-chester-elton on 29 June 2017.

22. If you'd like to complete Hogan's 'Dark Side' assessment, you're welcome to contact me via www.leaderspace.com or go direct to www.hogan.com.

23. These statistics come from a review in J. Hogan, R. Hogan & R. B. Kaiser (2011) Management derailment. In S. Zedeck, Sheldon (Ed). *APA Handbook of Industrial and Organizational Psychology, Vol 3: maintaining, expanding, and contracting the organization,* pp555-575). Washington, DC, US: American Psychological Association. As the authors state, when commenting on a table showing the estimates across 12 published studies, "These estimates are remarkably consistent despite the fact that they come from distinctly different sources, including documented failure rates in publicly traded companies... estimates provided by senior executives from a variety of for-profit and non-profit organizations... estimates provided by organizational consultants... and estimates provided by organizational researchers".

24. I've drawn here on the Thomas-Kilmann Conflict Inventory and S. Spencer (2004) *The Heart of Leadership.* London: Rider. Other influences include Dotlich & Cairo (*op. cit.*) and the 'OK Corral' from Transactional Analysis.

25. I'm heavily influenced here by what Bill Torbert calls 'action logics'. See, for instance, D. Fisher, D. Rooke & B. Torbert (2003) *Personal and Organisational Transformations through Action Inquiry.* Edge/Work Press.

26. Don't worry, I can do the maths! Obviously not everyone does a 50-hour working week and there are 60 minutes, not 50, in a one-hour meeting. However, I have never attended a one-hour meeting that started and finished bang on time with no time wasted, so I've opted for a rounder number based on an estimated 50 minutes of useful time in a meeting. I'd say that's fairly generous.

27. See, for instance, A. Ronaldson, G. J. Molloy, A. Wikman, L. Poole, J-C. Kaski & A. Steptoe (2015) Optimism and Recovery After Acute Coronary Syndrome: a clinical cohort study. *Psychosomatic Medicine, 77 (3),* pp311–318

28. I totally made the last one up. At the same time, if you think about it, the standard way of finding out would be to ask people. Regardless of whether their positive vibes attract more friends, optimists are likely to *say* they have more friends than pessimists would. Pessimists would most likely have a higher threshold for counting people as friends, given their tendency to think the worst of people. They'd also be more likely to assume others think less of *them* than they actually do.

29. Examples include J. Collins (2001) *Good to Great: why some companies make the leap... and others don't.* London: Random House. M. Newman (2008) *Emotional Capitalists: the new leaders.* Chichester, W. Sussex: John Wiley & Sons. V. E. Frankl (2004) *Man's Search For Meaning: the classic tribute to hope from the Holocaust.* London: Rider.

30. C. Dweck (2017) *Mindset – Updated Edition: changing the way you think to fulfil your potential.* London: Robinson.

31. Arguably, the labels 'proactive' and 'reactive' are more about behaviours than mind-set. I've chosen these labels over the more technically accurate labels of 'high vs low self-efficacy' or 'internal vs external locus of control' to make life easier for non-psychologists reading this book, then attempted to use those two more technical concepts to construct the definitions of 'proactive' and 'reactive' in this context. Apologies to any fellow psychologists (and other readers) who find that frustrating. It's also worth noting that some psychologists argue that self-efficacy and locus of control refer to the same psychological construct. See T. A. Judge. A. Erez, J. E. Bono & C. J. Thoresen (2002). Are Measures of Self-Esteem, Neuroticism, Locus of Control, and Generalized Self-Efficacy Indicators of a Common Core Construct? *Journal of Personality and Social Psychology. 83 (3)*, pp693–710.

32. From page 13 of I. Chaleff (1995) *The Courageous Follower: standing up to and for our leaders.* San Francisco, CA: Berrett-Koehler.

33. *Ibid.*

34. 'Amygdala hijack' is a term apparently coined by Daniel Goleman in his D. Goleman (1996) *Emotional Intelligence: why it can matter more than IQ.* New York, NY: Bantam Books.

35. In S. Peters (2012) *The Chimp Paradox.* London: Vermilion.

36. Argued by many, including B. Kellerman (*op. cit.*), who references a host of proponents including the founding father of psychoanalysis Sigmund Freud.

37. These concepts originated in Will Schutz's work with US Navy submarine crews in the 1950s. See W.C. Schutz (1958) *FIRO: a three dimensional theory of interpersonal behavior.* New York, NY: Holt, Rinehart, & Winston.

38. If you'd like to complete one of the FIRO questionnaires for an assessment of your needs in these areas you can contact www.leaderspace.com, www.jcaglobal.com or www.opp.eu.com

39. This particular quote of his is from page 125 of L. J. Peter (1977) *Peter's Quotations: ideas for our time.* New York: William Morrow and Company.

40. See, for example, J. Arnold, C.L. Cooper & I.T. Robertson (1998) *Work Psychology: Understanding Human Behaviour in the Workplace.* London: Financial Times / Pitman Publishing.

41. A number of military intelligence agencies use the 'Collect, Collate, Interpret, Assess, Communicate' model, which are essentially the Assess and Align phase of my Five-Phase Framework.

42. The Mission Command framework, as the British Army calls it, was actually pioneered by the Prussian Army in the 1860s, as a response to humiliating defeats in two major battles with Napoleon. It wasn't adopted by the British until 1987. Ironically, it's been argued that Hitler's refusal to follow the core principles of Mission Command seriously undermined the German army's ability to operate effectively in the latter years of the Second World War. Apparently, and perhaps in part because of the cocktail of drugs he was taking, Hitler couldn't handle giving his people this amount of freedom. As the war dragged on, he grew increasingly controlling, to the extent that he insisted on personally micro-managing the deployment of tank reserves at Normandy. Time wasted waiting for Hitler's orders delayed the tank units' response which enabled the Allies to land on the beach and seize and secure critical positions. It was my friend Anton Horne who introduced me to the concept of Mission Control when I was first scoping this book and he was working for PwC. Anton spent many years as a leader and follower in the British Army. Another source referenced in this chapter was Colonel B. Watters (2002) *Mission Command – Mission Leadership (Creating the Climate for Maximising Performance) – A Corporate Philosophy.* Sourced from http://www.raf. mod.uk/pmdair/rafcms/mediafiles/225D11C3_5056_A318_A8AF63C0D16C7670. doc. on 16 June 2016. Where Hitler's relationship with drugs is concerned, see *The Guardian*'s article on Norman Ohler's book *Blitzed: Drugs in Nazi Germany*, available at https://www.theguardian.com/books/2016/sep/25/blitzed-norman-ohler-adolf-hitler-nazi-drug-abuse-interview, retrieved on 20 October 2016.

43. The intention behind the MVP (Minimum Viable Product) is to create a product that has the minimum features, quality and usability required to take the product to a market, or perhaps beta testers, in order to test the concept, its key assumptions and the ways its users interact with it.

44. These have their origins in Douglas McGregor's theories of human motivation and management. Since he came up with them in the 1960s, a whole host of people have reworked his thinking. What I've offered here blends what appear loosely to be two different ways of looking at these seven levels. See D. McGregor (1960). *The Human Side of Enterprise*, New York, McGrawHill.

45. Quoted on the inside cover of I. Chaleff (op. cit.). That Conable's words are offered in support of Chaleff's book doesn't, in my mind, detract from their truth and impact.

46. I've based these on a trawl of the internet and my own thinking. One popular source, though, is N. Kerth (2001) *Project Retrospectives: a handbook for team reviews.* New York, NY: Dorset House Publishing.

47. This is a term used by my friend and colleague Grant Morffew, who can no longer recall the source of the term but credits Ken Blanchard with the term 'leading at a higher level'.

48. L. Y. Sun, S. Aryee & K. S. Law (2007). High-Performance Human Resource Practices, Citizenship Behavior, and Organizational Performance: a relational perspective. *Academy of Management Journal, 50,* pp558–577. Like the following seven sets of sources, I owe this reference to Y. C. Wei (2014) The Benefits of Organizational Citizenship Behavior for Job Performance and the Moderating Role of Human Capital. *International Journal of Business and Management, 9 (7),* pp87-99.

49. T. D. Allen & M. C. Rush (1998) The Effects Of Organizational Citizenship Behavior on Performance Judgments: a field study and a laboratory experiment. *Journal of Applied Psychology, 83,* pp247–260. B. B. Vilela, J. A. Varela Gonzalez & P. F. Ferrin (2008). Person-Organization Fit, OCB and Performance Appraisal: evidence from matched supervisor-salesperson data set in a Spanish context. *Industrial Marketing Management, 37,* pp1005–1019.

50. Allen & Rush (*op. cit.*); Vilela et al (*op. cit.*).

51. Sun et al (*op cit.*). X. P. Chen. (2005). Organizational Citizenship Behavior: a predictor of employee voluntary turnover. In D. L. Turnipseed (Ed.), *Handbook of Organizational Citizenship Behavior* (pp435–454). New York: Nova Science. X. P. Chen, C. Hui & D. J. Sego (1998) The Role of Organizational Citizenship Behavior in Turnover: conceptualization and preliminary tests of key hypotheses. *Journal of Applied Psychology, 83,* pp922–931.

52. C. P. Lin (2008) Clarifying The Relationship Between Organizational Citizenship Behaviors, Gender, and Knowledge Sharing in Workplace Organizations in Taiwan. *Journal of Business & Psychology, 22,* pp241–250.

53. C. C. Lin & T. K. Peng (2010) From Organizational Citizenship Behavior to Team Performance: the mediation of group cohesion and collective efficacy. *Management & Organization Review, 6,* pp55–75.

54. P. D. Dunlop & K. Lee (2004) Workplace Deviance, Organizational Citizenship Behavior, and Business Unit Performance: the bad apples do spoil the whole barrel. *Journal of Organizational Behavior, 25,* pp67–80.

55. You could, of course, argue that good organisational citizens contribute to profitability purely by taking on more work than they are paid to do, so no one needs to be paid to do it. I'd argue that they're also looking for ways – outside of their official remit – to save the organisation money and make its activities more efficient and impactful. But for some research on the profitability front, see D. J. Koys (2001). The Effects Of Employee Satisfaction, Organizational Citizenship Behavior, And Turnover On Organizational Effectiveness: a unit-level, longitudinal study. *Personnel Psychology, 54,* pp101–114.

56. Y. C. Wei (*op. cit.*).

57. *Ibid.*

58. I. Chaleff (*op. cit.*).

59. From p63 of I Chaleff (*op. cit.*).

60. These were stories Greg Reed from HomeServe shared when discussing the cultural change he'd seen (some might say "helped engineer" at the organisation, during a customer contact conference run by Sabio on 23 February 2017. HomeServe subsequently kindly agreed for me to share them in this book.

61. See Chapter 9 of R. Boston, *ARC Leadership* (*op. cit.*).

62. See Chapter 2 of *ARC Leadership* (*op. cit.*).

63. Interestingly, "Considers integrity of paramount importance" is one of five "follower competencies and components" suggested in a paper by the US Air Force. See Lt Col S. M. Latour & Lt Col V. J. Rast (2004) Dynamic Followership: The Prerequisite for Effective Leadership. *Air and Space Power Journal, Winter*. Retrieved from http://govleaders.org/dynamicfollowership.htm on 17 Oct 2016.

64. Adapted from R. J. Lewicki, B. Polin & R. B. Lount Jr. (2016) An Exploration of the Structure of Effective Apologies. *Negotiation and Conflict Management Research, 9 (2),* pp177–196.

65. L. ten Brinke & G. S. Adams (2015) Saving Face? When emotion displays during public apologies mitigate damage to organizational performance. *Organizational Behavior and Human Decision Processes, 130,* pp1–12.

66. I'm drawing here on work by Ryan Fehr and Michele Gelfand at the University of Maryland, which draws on research in sociology, law and other disciplines to suggest three types of apology. I was drawn to this by C. Jarrett (2010) How to apologise. *Psychologist, 23 (10)* p798.

67. D. De Cremer, M. M. Pillutla & C. R. Folmer (2011). How Important Is An Apology

To You? Forecasting errors in evaluating the value of apologies. *Psychological Science*, 22(1), pp45-48

68. Here I'm looking to take us beyond the great foundations laid by R. E. Kelley (1988) In praise of followers. *Harvard Business Review, 66,* pp142-148.

69. Grant Morffew (*op. cit*)

70. A helpful expression used on page 10 of A. Watkins (2016) *4D Leadership: competitive advantage through vertical leadership development.* London: Kogan Page.

71. Since finishing *The Boss Factor*, a colleague and I have started work on a book on this topic, as much of the literature is quite abstract and esoteric and we're keen to make it more accessible and practical. Good starting points, though, include Fisher, Rooke & Torbert (*op. cit.*); E. Jaques (1986) The Development of Intellectual Capability: A Discussion of Stratified Systems Theory. *The Journal of Applied Behavioral Science, 22 (4)*, pp361-383.

72. A term used on page 65 of *ARC Leadership (op. cit.)*.

73. R. Boston, R. Stevens & B. Cooke (2017) *'Focus on your strengths': is it guff?* Available at http://tinyurl.com/RB-RS-BC-strengths

74. My friend and mentor Professor Peter Hawkins has used this term in our various conversations over the years.

75. One useful source here is D. Dunning (2003) *Introduction to Type and Communication*. Palo Alto, CA: CPP, Inc. Alternatively, if you or someone you know is qualified in the Myers-Briggs, you can access a 'quick guide' looking at how different personality types prefer to use and receive email here: https://www.opp.com/en/Quick-Guide-to-effective-email-and-your-personality retrieved on 3 July 2017.

76. Apparently, the expression "Prior Planning and Preparation Prevents Poor Performance" and its derivatives have their origins in the British Army. I'm not sure anyone truly knows the source anymore.

77. If you're interested in distinctions between 'dialogue' and 'debate', you'll find a simple table in the resources section at www.leaderspace.com, where you'll also find other documents to support you and your team in delivering on the lessons in this book.

78. The Zig-Zag model focuses on the middle two 'functional pairs' within the Myers-Briggs framework: 'Sensing and Intuition' and 'Thinking and Feeling'. The argument is that any robust decision will draw fully on both sides of each of those two pairs, where individuals and teams will usually favour one side over the other – Sensing or Intuition to gather the data, then Thinking or Feeling to decide on the best course of action. A Sensing preference privileges the past and

present ways of doing things, and hard data, whereas a preference for Intuition favours broad themes, interconnections and future possibilities. A Thinking preference favours task focus, efficiency and equal, dispassionate treatment for all; a feeling preference takes individual differences into account, brings values into the equation and attends to the impact of the decision on relationships. Truly effective decision-making will take the best of all four perspectives, rather than being biased towards an individual or team's favourite two – zig-zagging from Sensing questions about the problem (e.g. "What does the data tell us?", "What's the history behind this problem?" and "What have we already tried?") to Intuition questions that open up the problem and potential options (e.g. "What's the bigger picture?", "What are the interconnections and interdependencies?", "What would 'good' look like?" and "What's the most creative thing we could do here?"), then to logic-based Thinking questions (e.g. "What are our criteria for deciding between options?", "What are the pros and cons of each option?" and "What assumptions lie behind each option?"), and finally onto Feeling questions (e.g. "How do we ensure our decision is aligned with our values?", "How do we gain buy-in to the final decision?" and "How do we acknowledge and deal with anyone's sense of not being heard through this process or any outstanding, irreconcilable differences of opinion?"). There's a helpful guide to this process, although it doesn't use the term 'zig-zag' explicitly, on page 39 of I. Briggs Myers (2000) *Introduction to Type.* Oxford: OPP.

79.   I've drawn from a wide array of sources here, too many to attribute anything meaningfully to any one of them. However, the following served as a starting point and so deserves a mention. E. Devaney (2014) *The Pros & Cons of 7 Popular Organizational Structures.* From Hubspot's website, 23 December. Retrieved from https://blog.hubspot.com/marketing/team-structure-diagrams#sm.00000kf8aaqfydfp5sdmg07bb7cuy on 11 April 2017.

80.   M. Nink & J. Robison (2016) *The Damage Inflicted by Poor Managers.* Retrieved from http://www.gallup.com/businessjournal/200108/damage-inflicted-poor-managers.aspx?g_source=EMPLOYEE_ENGAGEMENT&g_medium=topic&g_campaign=tiles on 3 July 2017.

81.   Drawing on page 11 of I. Chaleff (*op. cit.*).

82.   The phrase "a prize worth fighting for" came from a conversation with one of my test readers. Apologies: I can't remember which but I think it was either Dave Tansley or Tony Cooper.

83.   B. Tracy (2013) *Eat That Frog! Get More of the Important Things Done – sToday! London:* Hodder & Stoughton.

84. 'The Boston-Miah paradigm' emerged from a conversation with Helal Miah, one of my best friends since 1993.

85. R. F. Baumeister & J. Tierney (2012) *Willpower: discovering our greatest strength.* London: Allen Lane. K. McGonigal (2012) *Maximum Willpower: how to master the new science of self-control.* London: Macmillan.

86. W. Schutz (*op. cit.*). The labels I've used here are a combination of Schutz's original labels in the FIRO-B instrument and the more 'business friendly' labels recently introduced by the instrument's publishers CPP. The former precede the first 'slash' in my text; the latter follow.

87. My questions here are based on Jungian Type models of personality, the most successful being the Myers-Briggs Type Indicator (MBTI).

88. A major source of inspiration when I first started working on influencing styles was The Mind Gym (2005) *The Mind Gym.* London: Time Warner. Another has been the Myers-Briggs framework.

89. *ARC Leadership* (*op. cit.*).

90. S. Jeffers (2007) *Feel The Fear and Do It Anyway (20th anniversary edition).* London: Vermilion (Random House).

91. From page 14 of R. E. Kelley (2008) Rethinking Followership. In R. E Riggi, I. Chaleff & J. Blumen-Lipman (Eds). *The Art of Followership: how great followers create great leaders and organizations.* San Francisco, CA: Jossey-Bass

92. I took some inspiration for this section from Ira Chaleff (*op. cit.*).

93. My commitment vs courage grid is very closely aligned to the work of R. E. Kelley (2008, *op. cit.*). Barbara Kellerman's (*op. cit.*) five types of follower are differentiated in terms of the level of engagement they display (from disenfranchised isolates, through inactive bystanders to die-hards who're willing to give their lives for the cause). Her types, I believe, map onto my 'commitment' axis. Ira Chaleff (*op. cit.*) calls for courageous followership, although he weaves in responsibility as well, so his work weaves across both of my two axes.

94. R. E. Kelley (2008, *op. cit.*).

95. This is clear in the literature. For example, John S. McCallum names loyalty as one of seven essential qualities of a good follower and research by the US Air Force lists it as one of five "competencies or components". See, respectively, J.S. McCallum (2013) Followership: the other side of leadership. *Ivey Business Journal, Sept/Oct* (retrieved from http://iveybusinessjournal.com/publication/ followership-the-other-side-of-leadership/ on 3 July 2017) and Lt Col S. M. Latour & Lt Col V. J. Rast (2004) Dynamic Followership: the prerequisite for effective leadership. *Air and Space Power Journal, Winter*, pp102-110.

96. Page 11 of I. Chaleff (*op. cit.*).

97. For a detailed telling of the story, check out Chapter 6 of Kellerman (*op. cit.*).

98. I'm grateful to Seb Henkes for the sergeant major and World Cup examples. Seb was the co-founder and managing director of Sabio and a client of mine before he became a friend. He's a great example of a leader who sees the importance of creating a culture that enables effective followership.

99. There's a whole chapter on this in *ARC Leadership*, so it's hard to do all of those forces justice here.

100. R. Biswas-Diener (2012) *The Courage Quotient: How science can make you braver.* San Francisco, CA: Jossey-Bass.

101. Impostor syndrome was first described in print by psychologists in 1978. It's when a high-achieving individual is plagued by a persistent fear that someone will eventually discover that they're not as good as everyone thinks they are. Depending on which research paper you read, this fear of being exposed as a fraud seems to plague 40-70% of people. Some feel it consistently throughout their lives; others for shorter periods of time. P.R. Clance and S.A. Imes (1978) The imposter phenomenon in high achieving women: dynamics and therapeutic intervention. *Psychotherapy: Theory, Research and Practice, 15 (3)*, 241–247.

102. This concept comes from the work of Susan Scott, who encourages us to ask "What am I practising?" when we're acting less than courageously. She's taken the principle from a master (or 'sensei') of the Japanese martial art aikido, who observed that we are always "practising" something. To get into the neuroscience, repetition strengthens our neural pathways. To give you an analogy: deeply ingrained habits operate through signals passing along major six-lane highways in the brain. A new behaviour creates a new, small country lane – an alternative route that will initially be less attractive when we're in a hurry. Repeating that new behaviour again and again gradually widens that country lane, with the behaviour becoming easier each time, until that country lane becomes a six-lane highway in its own right. At that point, the old highway becomes defunct, the grass grows over it and we're left with a new, healthier habit. See S. Scott (2009) *Fierce Leadership: a bold alternative to the worst 'best practices' of business today.* London: Piatkus.

103. *Ibid.*

104. I. Chaleff (*op. cit.*).

105. These recommendations draw on a range of sources including common sense, my own unpublished work on influencing and work on courage in *ARC Leadership* (*op. cit.*), I. Chaleff (*op. cit.*), and B. Kellerman (*op. cit.*). Other sources include J. L. Badaracco, Jr. (2002) *Leading Quietly: an unorthodox guide to doing*

the right thing. Boston, Massachusetts: Harvard Business School Press and; R. Heifetz, A. Grashow & M. Linsky (2009) *The Practice of Adaptive Leadership: tools and tactics for changing your organisation and the world.* Boston, Mass: Harvard Business Press. Attributing individual recommendations to specific sources would be failing to recognise the interwoven nature of authors' ideas when it comes to 'speaking truth to power'. At the same time, it would be remiss of me to underplay the disproportionate influence Chaleff's work has had on these recommendations.

106. You'll find this list and other ideas on pages 90-91 of I. Chaleff (*op. cit.*).

107. A. Murray (2007) After the revolt, creating a new CEO. *The Wall Street Journal, May 5–6,* pages A1 & A10. Cited in B. Kellerman (*op. cit.*).

108. Specifically pages 135-146 of Heifetz, Grashow & Linsky (*op. cit.*).

109. A. Murray (*op. cit.*). Cited in B. Kellerman (*op. cit.*).

110. Gale Ann Hurd brought us The T*erminator and Terminator 2, Aliens, The Abyss, Armageddo*n and – sadly – two dreadful films about The Incredible Hulk. The quote is lifted from her keynote at the 2016 South by Southwest conference. Retrieved from https://youtu.be/KGFyNYWJnGg on 5 April 2017 (the quote comes at around 17 minutes in).

111. In 1998, a huge and hugely influential piece of research told us interviews were far less effective than we thought when it came to deciding which candidates are best suited to a particular job. More recently, one of the original authors updated their findings using more advanced (meta-analytic) techniques. Sadly, this potentially game-changing update didn't receive nearly as much attention as the original. The two studies, respectively, are F. L. Schmidt & J. E. Hunter (1998). The Validity and Utility of Selection Methods in Personnel Psychology: practical and theoretical implications of 85 years of research findings. *Psychological Bulletin, 124,* pp262-274; and F. L. Schmidt, I-S. Oh & J. A. Shaffer (2016, working paper) *The Validity and Utility of Selection Methods in Personnel Psychology: practical and theoretical implications of 100 years of research findings* (retrieved from https://www.researchgate.net/publication/309203898_ The_Validity_and_Utility_of_Selection_Methods_in_Personnel_Psychology_ Practical_and_Theoretical_Implications_of_100_Years_of_Research_Findings on 13 April 2017). The actual statistics appear at https://home.ubalt.edu/ tmitch/645/articles/2013-PTC-DCTalk-abstract%20and%20Tables%20%20 Refs%2011-06.doc (retrieved on 13 April 2017)

Lightning Source UK Ltd.
Milton Keynes UK
UKHW02f1205040118
315183UK00011BA/357/P